CAREERS IN COUNSELING AND GUIDANCE

CAREERS IN COUNSELING AND GUIDANCE

SHELLEY C. STONE
BRUCE SHERTZER
Purdue University

HOUGHTON MIFFLIN COMPANY BOSTON
New York Atlanta Geneva, Illinois Dallas Palo Alto

Printed in the U.S.A.

Library of Congress Catalog Card Number: 72–185792

ISBN: 0–395–13494–3

PREFACE

Our major purpose in writing this book is to present the career opportunities which are available in the fields of counseling and guidance. It will become evident to the reader that the term *counseling* is used in a broad sense, as it is an activity carried out in many settings and under diverse conditions. This book is designed for student use in beginning counselor education programs and as a supplementary source for persons seeking information about careers in this field.

We have tried, as fully as possible, to identify and include descriptions of many settings in which counseling can and does take place. In treating the field two factors make adequate coverage extremely difficult. The first of these involves an attempt to delimit a field that ranges widely in scope and personnel. The second problem stems from the uneven quality and quantity of information available about some settings and the counseling personnel employed in those settings. Added to these factors is the impossible task of including descriptions of innovative practices for which information has not yet been made generally available. Complete information is lacking, for example, about the many drug abuse programs which are springing up as this problem becomes an ever-increasing concern to society. Material about new approaches and practices in counseling is difficult to obtain because persons involved in such activities find it difficult to take time to write about them.

For the counseling areas covered, we have sought to include information concerning the setting itself, the nature of the services provided, the counselor's work, required preparation, working conditions, salaries and patterns of advancement, etc. Moreover, sources of further information are included for those who seek additional knowledge about specific settings and jobs.

We are grateful to many individuals for their assistance in preparing this manuscript, particularly the counselors who supplied descriptions of typical days at work. We also wish to thank Mrs. Nancy Holder for typing the manuscript, usually under adverse conditions.

Shelley C. Stone
Bruce Shertzer

CONTENTS

COUNSELING: A CAREER CHOICE

CHAPTER 1

What Is Counseling?

Counseling is a word used by many to describe what they do. Nevertheless, no one has ever been able to define it to the satisfaction of persons who claim it as their profession or who write about it. A possible definition of counseling is *an interaction process which facilitates an understanding of self and environment, and which results in changes in behavior and/or the establishment or clarification of goals for future behavior.* This definition probably would not be accepted by all counselors, as there are so many conflicting opinions in the field. The major problem in defining the word revolves around disagreement in the field as to the kind and extent of changes in behavior that can be expected as a result of counseling.

The common use of *counsel* to mean *advise* can be the cause of much conflict and confusion, since counselors in educational as well as other settings often insist they do not parcel out advice. Dictionary definitions of *counseling* stress advice and exchange of ideas, and *counselor* is usually designated as a legal adviser at an embassy, a lawyer, or a person in charge of children at a camp. To further obscure the issue, there are automobile salesmen and representatives from various brokerage firms, loan agencies, and mortuaries who bear such titles, respectively, as "investment counselor," "financial counselor," and "grief counselor"!

The lack of a clear definition of counseling stems from the fact that in its modern sense counseling is relatively new, and confusion and uncertainty are inevitable in any evolving field of study. Professional counseling organizations have, up until now, made few attempts to solve the problem. As the organizations mature, perhaps effort will be made to reduce confusion by defining the function of a person with the title of "counselor."

A few statements about the nature of counseling may help to clarify what it means:

1. In counseling, a personal relationship is involved that is characterized by warmth, understanding, and acceptance.

2. While in the past it was viewed as a one-to-one relationship, counseling today often involves small groups of people.

3. Counseling is a *process*—a phenomenon which shows continuous change over time. This implies that counseling is not a single event but involves sequential actions and practices directed toward a goal.

4. The counselor is usually viewed as a professional, as older or more mature, and as possessing specialized knowledge; his client may be troubled, anxious, upset, frustrated, but not necessarily emotionally disturbed.

5. The outcome of the counseling relationship is an improvement in client behavior. For example, the client makes a choice, increases his self-understanding, changes his attitudes, improves his relationships with others, feels more confident, etc.

What Does the Counselor Do?

The counselor devotes a large amount of his time to people. He works directly with people in an intimate, personal relationship to assist them in achieving their goals or improving their situation. To do this means that the counselor must learn to *listen*. To the counselor, listening does not mean just being quiet while he mentally prepares what he wants to say next; it means hearing what the other person is saying—and feeling—by attending to his verbal and nonverbal communications. Effective listening requires that the counselor interact with individuals on a person-to-person basis. These situations are usually emotionally taxing for both the counselor and his client.

Not all of the counselor's work with people is conducted in a one-to-one relationship. More and more counselors are conducting group counseling, or some form of intensive group experience such as sensitivity training, human relations training, encounter groups, or marathons. Usually six to twelve persons form a group, depending on its purpose.

It should be noted that the clientele of the counselor consists of "normal" individuals. Most severely emotionally disturbed persons are served by clinical psychologists or psychiatrists. The counselor works with individuals who experience situational, developmental, or identity problems. Such concerns can consist of choosing a future educational objective, an occupation, or marriage partner, or simply understanding oneself.

The counselor sometimes gives tests to help his client to understand himself better or to predict how well he might do in an educational or vocational venture. The tests usually include standardized group tests of ability, achievement, and vocational aptitude, as well as interest and personality inventories.

The counselor may teach mini-courses or micro-training laboratories lasting two to twelve hours. Such courses are usually organized according to the needs of the clientele served by the counselor. Topics might include "how to take a test," "how to apply for a job," or "how to get along with a teacher."

Some of the counselor's time is spent consulting with other persons in the same setting about the individuals the setting is designed to serve. For example, the school counselor meets with teachers about pupils in their classes, and the rehabilitation counselor talks with employers about handicapped persons he has placed.

The counselor's job includes knowing other specialists who also serve his clientele—physicians, psychologists, psychiatrists, mental health workers, welfare and social workers. He must know whom to contact if his work with a client indicates that a referral to another specialist is necessary and appropriate.

The counselor usually must devote a certain amount of his time to paperwork. While he may regard such work as routine and boring, it inevitably has to be done. It seems that few professionals are exempt from such work, and the counselor is no exception.

The following examples help to illustrate the situations of individuals who typically seek help from or are referred to a counselor. Much of the counselor's day-to-day work is spent in situations similar to the ones presented here.

John R., a 17-year-old high school senior, comes to the school counselor's office because he wants to go to college; he and his family have only $800 of the estimated $2,000 necessary to finance the first year.

Mary P., a 37-year-old mother of two children, comes to the employment counselor's office seeking a job. Her two children are both in school, and she is looking for a way to occupy her time. Prior to her marriage she had worked for three years as an inspector on a television assembly line but wishes to investigate other types of work.

Peter C., a 21-year-old combat veteran of Vietnam, seeks the help of a veterans' counselor because he wants to go to welding school.

Sam B., a 16-year-old high school dropout, has had his left hand mangled in a hay baler and was referred by a physician to the vocational rehabilitation counselor.

The X-Y-Z Dairy Distributing Company refers three men to a counselor in private practice for assessment and evaluation; one of the three is to be promoted to route supervisor.

Larry G., a 39-year-old prison inmate, requests the help of a counselor because he has not had a letter from his wife for nine weeks.

Ben A., a 21-year-old high school graduate comes to a counselor in a vocational training school because he is dissatisfied with his present job as a flagman on a highway construction crew.

Christine L., a 20-year-old single college student, tells her dormitory counselor that she must leave college. She believes that she is pregnant, since her period is three weeks overdue.

David and Sarah D., married for two years, were referred by David's lawyer to a marriage counselor when David sought legal advice about obtaining a divorce.

Rex E., an eight-year-old second-grader, was referred by his teacher because he has not talked in class since school opened four weeks ago.

Deborah F., a 14-year-old high school freshman, sees the counselor because her two best friends have smoked marijuana at the last two parties she attended with them.

How Does Counseling Differ From Psychotherapy, Psychiatry, and Psychoanalysis?

The above description of counseling is intended to help clarify to some extent what the counselor does. However, much confusion exists among the public about how counseling relates to psychotherapy, psychiatry, or psychoanalysis. Counseling is sometimes viewed erroneously as "psychoanalysis" of an individual. It should be emphasized that counselors are not psychoanalysts or psychiatrists, who practice psychotherapy, and few if any counselors with a year or so of graduate preparation view themselves as such. Some of the distinctions among these terms are identified and described briefly below.

Psychiatry is a medical specialty dealing with the diagnosis, prevention, and treatment of emotional disorders or defects. Originally the function of psychiatry was the medical care of the mentally ill. As the profession emerged and evolved, much of its treatment was not specifically medical, and many persons who were treated were not mentally ill or emotionally disabled. Thus, in practice, psychiatry is often indistinguishable from other specialties dealing with problems of emotional adjustment. Psychiatrists are licensed to practice medicine and thus can employ chemotherapy, shock therapy, and other medical methods. Their training has not traditionally emphasized the study of the psychology of "normal" people.

Psychoanalysis is a method for treating patients using the doctrines originally set forth by Sigmund Freud, or modified by one of his followers, which emphasize the concepts of unconscious motivation, conflict, and symbolism. With some exceptions, a psychoanalyst is usually a physician as well as a psychiatrist who treats neuroses (disorders characterized by anxiety, compulsions, obsessions, fugues, phobias, or motor and sensory manifestations such as tics) and a variety of other emotional disorders. While the boundaries of psychoanalysis are not sharply defined, preparation for practice includes the study of the unconscious, analytical psychology, and individual psychology according to Freudian thought or a modification of it.

Psychotherapy is a general term referring to the use of any psychological techniques to treat emotional disorders or maladjustment. Psychiatrists, clinical psychologists, counseling psychologists, and psychiatric social workers engage in psychotherapy. While the term is applicable to a wide range of psychological treatments, its use does not specify the severity of the problem, the duration and intensity of treatment, or the theoretical orientation of the practitioner.

Clinical psychology employs psychological knowledge and practice to help individuals to cope with behavioral disorders and to achieve improved personal adjustment and self-expression. Like psychiatrists, clinical psychologists are involved in the diagnosis, treatment, and prevention of emotional problems; but they do not use chemotherapy, shock therapy, or other medical methods.

Counseling psychology is one of the newest psychological specialties. Counseling psychologists are equipped to treat personal problems not classified as mental illness although they may be related either to emotional or physical illness. While the boundary between clinical and counseling psychology is not precise, usually counseling psychologists concentrate on transient situational or personal problems and neuroses. Their training internship, in contrast to that of clinical psychologists, is spent in settings other than mental hospitals.

Psychiatric social work deals primarily with the emotionally disturbed persons and their families. The preparation of psychiatric social workers specializes in diagnosing psychological, cultural, social, and economic factors influencing the patient's mental health and general outlook. Social workers in mental health clinics and hospitals help patients to deal with emotional and environmental problems. At the same time they assist the patient's family to understand emotional illness and to play a helpful part in creating a healthy psychological atmosphere within the family.

Counseling is an interacting relationship in which one person helps another to understand himself and his environment and to make voluntary changes in his behavior. Many methods are used in the counseling relationship to assist the individual in achieving self-understanding, in selecting courses of action, and in developing a healthy psychological environment. Counseling is closely related to psychotherapy, but the individual who receives counseling is not emotionally ill.

The common goal of persons in these various helping professions is to assist individuals in becoming fully functioning persons. Their primary means of extending assistance is through a *helping relationship* (see Chapter 2 for major characteristics of a helping relationship). In their work persons in these professions emphasize prevention, for they know that care and treatment are not enough—that causes must be uncovered.

The major differences among the professions lie in professional training, clientele, setting, and extensiveness of treatment. Two years of graduate work is generally required for psychiatric social work; two to four years beyond the medical degree for psychiatry; while psychoanalysis, as a specialty within psychiatry, requires an additional two to four years of preparation. A fully qualified counseling or clinical psychologist usually possesses a doctoral degree. Two years of graduate study is now the established professional standard for school counseling personnel, although many counseling practitioners in schools and noneducational settings have completed only one year beyond the bachelor's degree. The emphasis on certain content areas in preparation programs may be more important than the length of training. Preparation for psychiatric and clinical psychology usually focuses on behavioral pathology and personality evaluation, while training for counseling psychology and counseling emphasizes total development of the "normal" personality and developmental behavior.

Psychiatry and psychotherapy as professions usually imply a "deeper" involvement with the individual's personality, since they are concerned more with serious behavioral conditions. On the other hand, the counseling relationship is likely to be less intense emotionally than psychotherapy. Psychotherapy usually extends over a long period of time because of the focus on personality reorganization, whereas counseling is conducted in a more limited period of time. Psychiatrists and clinical psychologists usually are employed in hospital settings; counseling psychologists and psychiatric social workers frequently practice in community settings; and counselors are found predominantly in educational settings. However, it should be noted that in all the professions the setting is characterized by variety.

What Is the Counselor Like?

A policy statement endorsed by the American Personnel and Guidance Association, the professional organization for counselors, has stated that the counselor should have six basic qualities: (1) a belief in each person as an individual, (2) a commitment to individual human values, (3) an alertness to the world, (4) open-mindedness, (5) self-understanding, and (6) professional commitment. Most practicing counselors would say that they hope to attain these ideal qualities. In reality, the counselor is a person who possesses some of the human weaknesses common to all of us.

Much research has been conducted during the past 20 years to determine how the counselor differs from the non-counselor in such characteristics as ability, interests, and personality traits. In a number of studies counselors have been compared to teachers, school administrators, engineering students, clinical psychology students, and college students in general.

Some of the research studies demonstrate that counselors often score high on (1) social service scales of interest inventories, and (2) nurturance, intraception, and affiliation scales of personality measures. Research efforts also have been directed toward establishing the characteristics of the "good" versus the "poor" counselor. The research literature is often confusing because the results are inconsistent, fragmentary, and elusive. The fact that the traits of counselors vary so widely, and that one trait interacts with another, makes a single listing of such characteristics useless. Moreover, it is not necessarily important to inquire whether a counselor possesses certain traits, but whether these traits are operative within the actual counseling situation.

Although listing desirable traits of the counselor is of questionable value, a few salient personal qualities of the "good" counselor are described below.

1. *Tolerance for ambiguity.* A counselor who possesses this quality is willing to accept situations that are uncertain or that do not yield easily to his understanding and control. Not only is he willing to accept such situations, but he feels comfortable knowing that everything cannot be reduced to black and white. This personal trait, the opposite of authoritarianism and rigidity, seems to enable the counselor to work with an individual without resorting to external sanctions or pat solutions in order to resolve, explain, or simplify complicated situations.

2. *Acceptance of self.* A person possessing this quality has an objective and unemotional recognition of his abilities and limitations, his virtues and faults without an undue sense of alienation, pride, or guilt. Because he views his personal qualities as worthy, he is not inclined to be passive. Rather, his acceptance of what he is enables him to extend constructive efforts in behalf of others. A counselor who has attained some degree of self-acceptance has no need to "use" his clients to satisfy personal needs for self-esteem.

3. *Interest in people.* A counselor who cares for people responds to others in ways that promote personal interaction. He wants to be involved with and work with people whom he views as capable individuals, not objects to be manipulated. He is a humanist with a positive rather than pessimistic attitude toward people.

4. *Willingness to experiment, change, and improve.* A counselor with this quality seems to express it not only toward others but toward himself. His adaptability enables him to change his own behavior without undue stress or friction. He seeks to grow, to explore, and to try out new behavior and means of personal expression.

5. *Intelligence.* Counselors must possess sufficient verbal and quantitative ability to reason and solve problems with logic and perception. This does not mean that counselors must be in the top 1 percent of the population in intellectual ability, but it does mean that they are above average in intelligence. They have to have sufficient capability to survive graduate school work. Good verbal ability seems to be an important attribute, since counseling is a "thinking" and "talking" occupation.

In summary, perhaps it can be said that counselors generally are likable individuals with whom people feel free to talk.

Where Does the Counselor Work?

Counselors are employed in a variety of settings, although currently the largest number by far is employed in secondary schools. It is estimated that approximately 40,000 counselors currently work in high schools. During the late 1960's elementary schools began to employ counselors, and by 1971 it was estimated that about 6,000 counselors were at work in that setting.

Most colleges and universities extend counseling services to their students. In addition, they employ individuals to conduct student personnel services in admissions, registration, financial aid, and placement. Counselors are employed by vocational and technical schools and by institutions which offer adult education programs.

Not all counselors are located in educational settings. The U.S. Employment Service, the Veterans Administration, and the Vocational Rehabilitation Administration all employ a sizable number of counselors. Special governmental programs for the disadvantaged number counselors among their personnel. Counselors are employed in community agencies, prisons, and some mental hospitals. A few go into private practice.

Today's counselor can virtually choose the setting and the clientele in which he is most interested. Counseling in these various settings is described more fully in Chapters 3, 4, and 5.

What Does It Take To Be a Counselor?

This question can best be answered in two parts. The first part describes the education required to be a counselor, while the second part discusses the qualities a counselor needs for survival in his profession.

EDUCATIONAL REQUIREMENTS

Essentially, counselor preparation in the United States takes place at the graduate level. An individual can earn the master's or doctoral degree with counseling as the major area of concentration. At present a small number of universities offer a two-year program leading to a master's degree in counseling. Most employers require that a counselor have completed a minimum of one year of graduate education or the master's degree.

Approximately 400 universities in this country prepare counselors. The graduate programs they offer differ considerably in quality, direction, resources, and scope. Some are "one-man" departments in which a single person teaches all the courses and supervises all of the trainees' experiences. Obviously, one-man programs leave much to be desired insofar as quality in counselor education is concerned.

Only a few graduate programs specify certain courses which must be taken at the undergraduate level before admission to counselor training programs. However, many professors in counselor preparation programs urge undergraduates to take as much coursework in the behavioral and social sciences as possible, including psychology, sociology, anthropology, and economics. A number of practicing counselors have completed programs of teacher preparation at the undergraduate level.

The American Personnel and Guidance Association specifies that the entry-level counselor should have developed, as a result of his preparation, understanding and competence in the following areas:

1. the foundations and dynamics of human behavior and of the individual in his culture;
2. philosophy and principles underlying counseling and other personnel services;

3. the nature and range of human characteristics and methods of appraising them;
4. vocational development theory;
5. educational and vocational information—its nature and uses;
6. counseling theory and practice;
7. statistics and research methodology as well as familiarity with electronic data-processing and information-gathering;
8. group counseling procedures and practices;
9. professional relationships and ethics;
10. supervised counseling experiences provided through laboratory, practicum, and internship activities;
11. knowledge of the employment setting.

It is our opinion that the above statement of areas in which the counselor is expected to achieve understanding and competence applies not just to counselors in educational settings but to all entry-level professional counselors.

During the past few years, some government agencies and educational institutions have employed counselor-aides, or paraprofessionals, who do not possess the master's degree in counseling. A few individuals have been employed successfully as counselor-aides without having attended college. While opportunities for entering the counseling profession at this level are not very great at present, it is anticipated that openings will increase during the next few years.

OTHER CRITERIA

The above paragraphs outline the educational requirements for becoming an entry-level counselor. Some of the personal qualities of the counselor have been identified earlier in this chapter. A few criteria drawn from our personal experience should also be mentioned.

1. The counselor must be emotionally strong. Not infrequently the counselor's work brings him into contact with individuals whose life situations are characterized by hopelessness, despair, and maltreatment by others—problems which are sometimes insoluble. The easy reaction is to "bleed" a little for such individuals and to forget them quickly. But the counselor cannot take the easy route, for counseling means more than tears and sympathy; it requires helping individuals to find the personal and external resources to help themselves.

In addition, the counselor must be strong enough emotionally to withstand criticisms of his work (see Chapter 2 for a discussion of these criticisms). A few persons in the helping professions and the public at large may charge that he lacks the professional competence needed for his work. Many view the counselor's efforts as unnecessary or as merely serving to encourage weakness and dependence in persons who lack the strength to manage their own lives. However, most people who make this charge never pay much attention to the good results achieved by the counselor.

2. *A counselor cannot care too much about status and prestige.* Counselors are usually ranked near the bottom in most prestige surveys of helping professionals. A person who is greatly interested in his position in the "pecking order" or who has a need for deference from others would be happier in some other occupation.

3. *Counseling is not a nine-to-five job.* The counselor often must work evenings and early mornings in order to see clients who cannot come during regular office hours. Sometimes a client will telephone late at night with an emergency situation that requires attention. In addition, outside activities may consume a large portion of the counselor's day. Community organizations need and demand a counselor's commitment, time, and energy.

4. *Preparation for counseling does not end with the master's or doctoral degree.* There are university courses and other educational offerings the counselor must take if he is to continue to learn and develop both personally and professionally. He will want to keep up with the current research through books and articles in professional journals.

5. *It is essential for the counselor to examine and to be aware of his own values.* He has to know what he believes in and why he believes it in order to be an effective counselor. At the same time he must be able to permit other people to examine their values and work out what is right and im-

portant for them—even if their beliefs and solutions do not mirror his own.

6. *The counselor must be able to keep a healthy perspective.* Because he often spends a considerable amount of time with individuals who are distressed or emotionally troubled, the counselor's perspective of man often becomes distorted. He must frequently remind himself of what most individuals are like rather than view the world through the eyes of his troubled clients.

7. *Activities and experiences have to be well planned to avoid becoming a "culturally encapsulated" counselor.* C. Gilbert Wrenn, a noted author, educator, and counselor, has explained that cultural encapsulation involves living in a "cocoon of pretended reality—a reality which is based upon the past and the known, upon seeing that which is as though it would always be so." A person can become encapsulated within his own culture or subculture, or within the pretense that the present will always endure. To avoid encapsulation, the counselor must guard against believing that what he regards as truth is immutable. He can do so through re-examining his own beliefs. Moreover, he must question whether as a counselor he may draw safely from his own educational and vocational experience. Flexibility of thought can be developed through travel, by talking with people whose ideas are different from his, and by questioning something which he believes but which other people of integrity reject.

8. *Counseling is not the quickest road to wealth.* A person whose life objective is to make money should forget about counseling as an occupation. (More information about the counselor's salary will be given in the following section on economic gains.)

9. *A counselor cannot believe or behave as if he has "saved" his client.* The counselor provides only the conditions and environment in which clients change certain behaviors —not the change itself. A counselor can help the counselee to obtain certain goals, but he cannot do it for him. It follows, then, that effusive thanks and praise for his efforts will be rare. This does not mean that his efforts are unrecognized by clients, but simply that the reward the counselor receives is the development of independence and healthy functioning

in his client. The counselor is rewarded when his client becomes capable of autonomous, responsible self-management.

10. *Not all of the counselor's work, even client contacts, is necessarily dramatic or exciting.* Many of the problems presented by clients become repetitive to the experienced counselor, but never routine. Each new individual the counselor works with is experiencing his own personal concerns. Yet in their development individuals do engage in many similar life experiences and decision-making situations. No matter how many times the counselor has dealt with the same problem, he cannot react patronizingly or in a way which conveys that "this is just a stage you are passing through," or "others have surmounted such a common problem."

11. *The counselor is not successful with every client.* When he starts working with a client he expects to be helpful, but in some cases he inevitably experiences failure. This may result from any of several reasons. Sometimes the counselor is ineffective because of his own shortcomings. On the other hand, clients are not always ready or willing to pay the emotional price to change, even though they ask for help. Many come for help expecting things to be done for them and are unable to use the experience to accomplish change in themselves.

What Are the Counselor's Rewards?

The last section described the requirements needed to become a counselor and some of the realities in the field. Here, the focus will be the economic and personal gains and satisfactions inherent in the counselor's work.

ECONOMIC GAINS

Counseling is rarely a high-income occupation. Generally the salary is related to the amount of training, as in other fields. The salary range of a counselor with a master's degree is between $7,500 and $11,000, depending on his experience and the setting in which he is employed. If the counselor has a doctorate he generally earns from $9,000 to $16,000, depending on experience and setting.

While these salary estimates may appear highly attractive, many professionals with equivalent preparation (such as physicians, dentists, or engineers) earn considerably more, once established. It should be kept in mind that most counselors are employed in nonprofit, social institutions—schools, community agencies, or government agencies. Social institutions either are heavily subsidized by public funds or at best attempt to break even financially. As in most types of work, the rewards and satisfactions of counseling depend largely on the person's motives for entering the profession and on the ability of the occupation to meet his psychological needs.

PERSONAL GAINS

Personal gains are sometimes jokingly called "psychic income." Even though psychic income does not pay the bills, it cannot be dismissed lightly. Occupational theorists for years have advised that the further one moves up the occupational ladder from routine manual labor, the less important economic factors become and the less they influence job satisfaction.

Presumably a major source of job satisfaction for the counselor is the sense of satisfaction that arises from meeting his own psychological needs. While it is difficult to catalog the needs of the counselor that can be met through this type of work, certainly they include working with people, helping others, engaging in psychological "intimacy" with others, and responding to challenging human problems. These factors and others provide the motivation for entering the field and are a continual source of satisfaction in the counselor's work.

Another attraction of counseling is that it is a relatively young and dynamic field of work. Unlike some professions which are overlaid with tradition, counseling as a profession is fluid and developing. There is much room for innovation, creativity, and variety of approach in practice. Many people find these conditions essential to having a viable and exciting career.

In our own experience we have found that the counselor's greatest satisfaction comes through extending constructive assistance to others. He is usually aware of his successes, and every small triumph in his client's progress provides him with great satisfaction.

COUNSELING: A HELPING PROFESSION

CHAPTER 2

Treatment is given in this chapter to the development of counseling, why counseling may be viewed as a helping profession, and some of the characteristics associated with the helping relationship. Attention is then directed to identifying and describing some of the major criticisms of counseling and counselors. Finally, some issues and trends in counseling are set forth.

How Did Counseling First Begin?

The answer to how counseling first began depends at least partly on one's point of view. Some would say that counseling, loosely defined, occurred whenever one man turned to his fellow for help or support or when he received advice.

Counseling as a profession is still a very young field. It may be some time before an historical analysis is written of the policies and personalities in counseling which formed the sources of its ideas and principles. At present few attempts have been made to do more than chronicle the developments that have occurred during the 65 years or more that counseling has existed as a profession. A comprehensive history might reveal some lessons from the past to guide future development in counseling. Certainly the profession could benefit from a more thorough understanding of the forces that have produced the development of counseling.

ORIGINS OF COUNSELING

It is difficult to pinpoint the establishment of counseling as a profession. However, it is usually attributed to Frank Parsons, who in 1908 founded the Vocational Bureau in Boston. Later to become part of Harvard University, the Vocational Bureau was established to assist young men and women in making vocational choices based on their interests and aptitudes. Parsons, often called the "father of guidance," also established the first counselor-training program to prepare counselors for vocational bureaus he thought would be established and maintained by schools, colleges, business and professional associations, and the YMCA. Parsons died in late 1908. His book, *Choosing a Vocation,* was published posthumously in 1909 presenting his ideas on the kind of helping relationship he felt was needed.

Important contributions to the development of counseling came from Jessie B. Davis, who from 1898 to 1907 devoted a considerable portion of his time to counseling eleventh-grade students at Central High School in Detroit, Michigan. When he became principal in 1907 of the Grand Rapids High School, he initiated a school-wide program of character development and vocational information. Other school districts around the country followed the lead of the Grand Rapids program and employed counselors to assist students in educational and vocational planning and placement. Programs were started in Cincinnati, Salt Lake City, Providence, and Lincoln, Nebraska.

During 1908–1909 Eli B. Weaver of the Boys' High School of Brooklyn achieved national prominence through his efforts to organize counseling services in New York City schools. Weaver was the leading force behind the New York City Vocational Guidance Survey of 1911. In addition, Weaver was instrumental in organizing several local agencies to offer counseling and job placement. He promoted the Second National Conference on Vocational Guidance held in New York City in 1912.

HISTORICAL FORCES AND FACTORS

It seems fairly certain that in this country counseling was first begun to assist individuals with vocational problems. If in fact its origin was not in an educational setting, it was quickly adopted by the schools, and its early important developments were associated with them. Its inception in the early 1900's was not accidental, for the period was full of powerful social reform movements. Vigorous attacks were mounted against a number of social ills: big business combines, the selfish policies of certain businessmen, corrupt scheming between businessmen and governmental officials, control by the railroads of rural politics and economic life, depletion of the natural resources, the inequality of bargaining power between workers and employers, the treatment of immigrants, city slums, oppressive child labor practices. The beginnings of counseling are lodged within this outcry for sweeping humanitarian and social reforms. Additional factors and forces aiding the development of counseling are summarized briefly below.

1. *The mental hygiene movement.* Stimulated by Clifford Beers' book, *A Mind That Found Itself*, the National Committee for Mental Hygiene was founded in 1909. In his book Beers described his personal confinement in a mental hospital and aroused public reaction to the deplorable conditions that characterized these institutions. Although initially organized to promote the improvement of services to the mentally ill, the national mental health organization soon stressed the preventive aspects of mental health. Since it was known that mental illness could be treated more effectively if identified early in life, mental hygienists encouraged educators to become more sensitive to the deep insecurities and the lack of identity prevalent among youth.

2. *The testing movement.* The development and use of standardized tests had a strong influence on counseling. Following Alfred Binet's work on the testing of individual intelligence and the construction of standardized group tests of ability during World War I, standardized achievement and ability testing grew rapidly in popularity. The testing movement was helpful to the development of counseling because it stressed that if one was to assist an individual, information about him must be gathered systematically and used intelligently.

3. *The child-study movement.* During the 1920's and 1930's, child-study centers, scientific journals, and organizations designed to promote the well-being of children came

into existence. The movement emphasized the individual as the focal point of study, the importance of the formative years for mature personality development, and the need for reliable, factual knowledge about children.

4. *Compulsory education.* After 1880, when the legal status of the high school was established as a free public institution, school enrollments increased substantially. As they did so, the curriculum was changed to meet the needs, interests, and abilities of a heterogeneous student population. Compulsory school attendance, improved child labor laws, and expanded curricula brought thousands of children into schools who sometimes had no desire to be there and who needed help to maximize their own abilities, to find their way through the school, and to adjust to society.

5. *Personnel work in industry.* Another development which influenced counseling was the beginning of personnel work in industry. With the introduction of job analysis techniques and the development of standardized group intelligence and aptitude tests, business and industry became more objective in selecting new employees.

6. *Federal government support.* The federal government, principally through the Departments of Labor and of Health, Education, and Welfare, helped to influence the development of counseling. Congress enacted legislation that established counseling in settings such as rehabilitation centers, community agencies, veterans agencies, schools and colleges. Substantial financial assistance has been given by the government for the preparation and employment of counselors in many settings.

7. *Professional Organizations.* The first national conference for counselors was conducted in Boston in 1910, followed in 1912 by a second one in New York. In 1913 the National Vocational Guidance Association was founded in Grand Rapids, Michigan. In 1952, the American Personnel and Guidance Association (APGA) was formed through the merging of several counseling and guidance professional associations. Currently APGA has eight divisions that serve to promote counseling and personnel work. The Division of Counseling Psychology (Division 17) of the American

Psychological Association has issued policy statements on counseling and has sponsored symposia at conventions. The professional organizations have promoted the development of counseling through their national, regional, and state conventions, local branches, and through their publications.

This brief overview of the beginnings of counseling serves to emphasize that its development has been a product of social and economic forces. Equally important has been the rise of individual psychology and its contribution to understanding and helping individuals. Individual rights, needs, and desires have traditionally been emphasized in America. Central among its values is that each person should have the opportunity to exercise his special abilities in a manner which is personally satisfying and socially useful.

Thus, the emergence of the counselor's role was an expression of our society's deep concern for the individual. Practicing counselors in every setting are charged with the awesome responsibility of assisting individuals in understanding themselves better and in adjusting to changing educational, vocational, and social conditions.

THE CURRENT STATUS OF COUNSELING

Counseling at present is an emerging profession with an unsteady growth rate. The decade of the 1960's was a period of rapid advance. Professional organizations attracted and held an unprecedented number of members. Professional journals and publications in the field increased exponentially. There was an incredible four-fold increase in counseling practitioners in comparison with past decades. The public's faith and acceptance of counseling were at a high level, and the counselor's skills were in demand by many sectors of the economy. Refinements and modification took place in counseling tools and techniques.

Yet despite the many changes that took place during the 1960's, counseling in the 1970's is bound to evolve in new directions. Struggles for power seem to be ever-present among counseling practitioners. Differences in opinion persist among factions of counselors as well as between counselors and other groups. It is highly probable that the need to define and alleviate these differences will lead to the emergence of new functions and new specialties. Certainly the need to communicate more effectively to the public and to other professionals about who the counselor is and what he does will require resourceful and able practitioners. Nevertheless, counselors with enthusiasm, competence, and sensitivity can build upon their profession's foundation.

What Is a Helping Profession?

A *helping profession* involves helping individuals through facilitating their personal development. Increasingly, counselors and therapists use this term to refer to what they do. Perhaps a brief explanation of each word in the term *helping profession* would be helpful.

DEFINITION OF PROFESSION

A profession is commonly defined as an occupation requiring training in the liberal arts or the sciences and advanced study in a specialized field. Such work usually does not involve manual labor. In early America, there were three recognized "learned" professions: teaching, law, and the ministry. Today, the list has expanded to include medicine, engineering, and many others. It is generally agreed that professionals are persons who

1. possess a common body of theoretical or specialized knowledge which has been codified, organized, and buttressed by research that can be communicated through higher education;
2. provide a unique vital social service, over which society has given them exclusive authority, that is applied to unstandardized but recurring problems;
3. act as a corporate group to assure minimum competence for entry into the occupation by establishing and enforcing standards for selection, training, and licensure;
4. have undertaken extensive specialized training to enter the occupation;
5. emphasize service to society rather than economic gain;
6. possess considerable if not complete autonomy in performing their social service;
7. follow a code of ethics in their standards of professional conduct;

8. constantly update their competence by keeping abreast of relevant technical research literature and by participating in meetings of the members.

DEFINITION OF HELPING

Definitions of *helping* are sufficiently broad to include many nurturing and uplifting contacts among people. Presumably bank clerks and politicians do not use the term to describe their work because their occupations, while providing beneficial services of an external nature, do not have the primary purpose of facilitating the individual's personal development. The helping professions engage in activities designed to assist others in understanding, modifying, or enriching their behavior so that growth takes place.

THE HELPING PROFESSIONS

In a sense any profession is a helping profession in that it performs a unique service for society. However, C. H. McCully has defined a helping profession "as one which, based upon its specialized knowledge, applies an intellectual technique to the existential affairs of others toward the end of enabling them to cope more effectively with the dilemmas and paradoxes that characterize the human condition."[1]

McCully defined existential problems as those requiring choice or decision but for which no sure external guide is readily available to provide a solution or answer. Further, he sought to make clear that existential problems were not limited to profound, ultimate questions but included everyday mundane situations such as choosing a college, occupation, or marriage partner.

Among the currently recognized helping professions are clinical psychology, social casework, and psychiatry. It is argued by some that counseling has not yet achieved all of the specified criteria to be considered a bona fide profession. However, because counseling occupations are moving toward professional status and because counselors exist to help others with their existential problems, counseling is viewed here as a helping profession.

[1] C. H. McCully, "Conceptions of Man and the Helping Professions." In Lyle L. Miller (Compiler) *Challenge for Change in Counselor Education* (Minneapolis: Burgess Publishing Company, 1969), p. 131.

What Are the Characteristics of a Helping Relationship?

Involvement with others in the form of a helping relationship is considered the heart of the helping professions. Such meaningful involvement produces the highest kind of human activity and challenges the best talents of helping professionals. Some essential qualities of the helping relationship are described below.

1. *The helping relationship is meaningful.* It is valued by the participants because it is personal, intimate, and relevant. The relationship is both anxiety-evoking and anxiety-reducing, and it involves mutual self-commitment.

2. *The helping relationship is an interpersonal process.* It is one in which two or more persons become reciprocally or mutually involved with each other. In their interaction they confront each other both verbally and nonverbally and are acutely aware of the other's presence. Both personalities have a marked effect on the total interaction process. The process is influenced by the way each participant views himself and the other person, his expectations about the experience, and his ability to communicate with the other person.

3. *The helping relationship takes place by mutual consent of those involved.* Individuals must want to be in the relationship in order for it to be effective. Consent is given explicitly or implicitly through choice, deference, or need. An individual cannot be coerced into a helping relationship; the absence of pressure is its hallmark.

The helping relationship must never be arbitrary or authoritative, for an individual compelled to be in such a relationship is less likely to think for himself, to grapple with his problems, or to try to discover the reasons why he behaves as he does.

4. *The relationship takes place because the individual to be helped needs understanding, advice, or some other form of assistance.* The individual comes for help because he "hurts" in some way. He feels distressed, anxious, or ineffective. He believes that he lacks the knowledge or com-

petence to deal with his situation. He *expects* the person from whom he seeks help to bring relief to his stressful situation. The person who extends help possesses special knowledge or competence and inspires confidence. He manifests sufficient skill, energy, and perceptiveness to induce and sustain trust, so that the individual to be helped is confident that he will be a stronger or better person than he was before. This confidence and trust in the helper is crucial to the helping relationship. The individual's faith, expectations, and confidence are basic ingredients in producing far-reaching changes in his behavior.

5. *The helping relationship is conducted through communication and interaction.* Each participant reacts and responds to the other verbally as well as nonverbally. Both parties convey or exchange knowledge, information, and feelings. The more lucid and articulate the communication between them, the more meaningful is the relationship.

In general, people spend a major portion of their time in some kind of interaction requiring skill in communication. In their everyday lives they are often successful in communicating their wants and needs to others. Yet to be really understood as an individual on a person-to-person basis is a complex, difficult, and often defeating experience. The person who extends help must listen to what is being said, catch underlying meanings, and fully attend to both verbal and nonverbal communication.

6. *The helping relationship has a structure.* Structure means a working arrangement, which begins when the helper and the person to be helped come together. Since the helper is more accustomed to interacting in such a personal manner, he initially assumes the responsibility for establishing and maintaining the relationship.

Many individuals who seek help often come with the belief that their role in the relationship is subordinate to the "expert" or helper. They conceptualize their part in the relationship as answering questions and providing information which the helper will utilize magically to correct their situation. Because of the preconceived attitudes and expectations a client often has, the helper usually provides an explanation of the part each is to play in the relationship.

Structure varies, depending on the type of helping relationship, but its essential features—patterns of stimuli and response—are always present. The clues and cues each person receives from the other determine ways of working together. The working relationship that is established depends on whether the helper wins the other's trust, confidence, and friendship. This working relationship is a unique, interpersonal experience in which qualities of warmth, trust, acceptance, and understanding are communicated and received by the client.

7. *The facilitative conditions in the helping relationship are empathic understanding, unconditional positive regard, and genuineness.* Many studies have emphasized that it is necessary for the helper (*a*) to be able to understand sensitively and accurately the individual who seeks help and to convey this understanding; (*b*) to communicate his warmth and respect for the person to be helped; and (*c*) to be integrated, mature, and genuine within the helping relationship. In other words, the helper must be able to sense the other's personal meanings as if they were his own, he must be genuinely himself, and he must accept the other person unconditionally as he is and as a person of worth. These conditions are essential to a successful helping relationship.

8. *Change is the objective of the helping relationship.* The participants learn from each other, and the experience results in change. The individual to be helped is different from what he was before the relationship. He no longer suffers as much; he is not as anxious; he is more aware of himself; he achieves more satisfying ways of behaving; he becomes a more mature person. Internal and external changes occur in his attitudes and actions, and in his perceptions of himself, others, and the world.

The foregoing characteristics have been abstracted from the literature describing a wide variety of occupations that can be grouped under the broad label of *helping professions*. Many counseling practitioners might differ as to the methods which should be used to implement these characteristics; however, most would agree in principle with the eight included above. While some of these characteristics may appear obvious to the reader, each must be present, at least to some degree, for the relationship to be facilitative and productive.

What Criticisms Are Made of the Counselor and Counseling?

Few fields of human endeavor are without their critics, and counseling is no exception. Charges have been leveled against the counselor personally as well as against the work he does. These criticisms range from superficial comments to highly serious charges. Some of the major ones will be outlined here.

A major criticism is that counseling is ineffective or superficial. This, of course, is a highly devastating charge, to which the counselor may become very defensive. All too often the counselor attempts to defend his work by claiming "too many clients and too little time." While there is little doubt that this is true and that it has some influence on what is achieved in counseling, such a defense begs the question.

Counseling has been challenged as ineffective by both informed and uninformed critics. Uninformed individuals sometimes make this charge because they do not understand the purposes or the processes of counseling. In many cases, the critics hold the opinion that seeking such specialized assistance represents a character defect, personal weakness, or mental illness. Although attitudes in the general public have shifted away from viewing individuals who seek help as "crazy" or "sick," there is little doubt that some of these perceptions are still operative. Uninformed and afraid, critics in the general public denigrate counseling from a base of sheer ignorance by denying that it has any value and by refusing assistance for themselves, even when they might benefit from it. Often they discourage their relatives or close friends from seeking such assistance. There is a tendency for many counselors to react to criticism at this level as if it did not deserve response. A better alternative is to present a nondefensive explanation directed toward educating such individuals as to why people seek help and the nature of the process.

The charge of ineffectiveness by informed critics is much more difficult for the counseling practitioner to counteract. Examination of the professional literature reveals that highly sophisticated, research-based criticisms abound within and without the field. While some progress has been made, the efforts of researchers to demonstrate the effectiveness of counseling leave much to be desired. This is especially true if one attempts to defend the activity using empirical research evidence. Paradoxically, research can be used either for or against counseling. As in other fields, studies exist which support as well as deny the benefits of counseling. However, few definitive research studies exist which support either the critics of counseling or its defenders.

Research in counseling is a complex and difficult task that rarely produces clear-cut findings. Even if the researcher can meet all or most of the demands required for an acceptable research design, he still may be unsuccessful. For in his attempt to study this complex area of human endeavor, he encounters a variety of counseling aproaches applied by a variety of practitioners to a variety of clients in various settings! Given such complexity it is small wonder that conflicting bits and pieces of findings emerge from such studies. The working counselor remains in the awkward position of having to defend his work against research-based charges with arguments based on studies that both criticize and support his activities. Although such conflicting evidence is a handicap to the counselor, a thorough knowledge of these studies will help him to answer his critics and to justify his efforts.

Undoubtedly, attempts will and should be made to demonstrate through research that counseling is of value. While this work goes forward, people will continue to seek and to benefit from professional help. The question will remain as to whether the subjective, positive reactions of clients are sufficient justification for the counselor's work.

Another criticism of the counselor is that he is too "soft" on his clients. Counseling is considered by some critics to discourage the strength of character required to survive in the tough, uncompromising world outside. This is a difficult charge to cope with, because the critic reacts from personal, internal attitudes and feelings which are directly contrary to the beliefs of most counselors. Probably the only useful reaction the counselor can have to this charge is to recognize that these critics are uninformed about the goals of counseling.

Ironically, the goals of the counselor do not differ from the values of the critic. Both desire strength of character, and both wish to help the individual to become autonomous and capable of dealing constructively with his life situation. The conflict appears to center around the means by which the goals are reached. Counseling can provide an alternative to the route of harsh and bitter experience which some view as essential to producing a tough, durable person. Advocates of the experience approach often overlook the fact that many persons may be destroyed or permanently damaged in the process. Undoubtedly, there are times in the lives of most individuals when they need and can benefit from assistance and active intervention by a sensitive, informed professional. To do less leads society back to the acceptance of "survival of the fittest" and the law of the jungle.

These comments are not meant to detract from the necessity for the counselor to be able to justify logically the steps he takes when he actively intervenes in a client's life. He must have solid reasons related to the well-being of the client when he, for example, changes a client's class schedule or protectively steps between a client and his family.

A third criticism of the counselor is that he is over-cautious in his work with clients who are considering educational or vocational ventures. Vocational counselors, particularly, have been charged with urging clients to consider only safe and secure positions, or with discouraging individuals from engaging in high-risk ventures.

A counselor's personal need for security ought not to be imposed on his client. And yet it is his obligation to assist the client to consider fully the reasons behind his choices and the ramifications of these decisions.

The criticism of over-caution may stem from a number of sources. It may be that the counselor's efforts to assist the client to consider thoroughly various alternatives are mistaken by the client for disapproval of a high-risk alternative. In addition, some of the critics who charge overcaution in vocational ventures may do so because they have a vested interest in securing personnel for specific occupational fields.

A fourth criticism charges that the counselor devotes his time and efforts to small "select" groups among the total clientele he claims to serve. In the schools, this sometimes takes the form of an over-emphasis on assisting college-bound students. In rehabilitation counseling, it can mean spending a disproportionate amount of time with clients who show the highest probability of benefiting from training and employment.

Some very human reasons may account in part for the validity of this criticism. For instance, a school counselor may devote the majority of his time to college-bound students because he knows and understands that type of student best, or because his clients have selected goals which have very positive sanctions in society, or because college-bound youth tend to be most adept in making use of the services and resources available to them. Counseling these students is attractive also because a criterion of the counselor's success is immediately available when the client is admitted to college. In rehabilitation counseling, it seems only natural that counselors would devote their time and effort to persons who are most likely to be rehabilitated. However, it would seem advisable for the counselor to have justifiable reasons for working with a subgroup among his clientele and to be aware that he is excluding others from the benefit of his services.

A fifth criticism to be dealt with is that the counselor is inadequately trained for his work. Often persons who level this charge have an exaggerated notion of what the counselor does or a narrow view of the kind of preparation needed to equip the counselor for his work.

Some psychiatrists take the view that without psychiatric training a person is not equipped to deal with human problems. These professionals would not (and should not) provide assistance for the types of problems many clients present to counselors. Extensive medical training is not, of course, required in order to deal effectively with many educational and vocational situations.

No self-respecting counselor attempts to work in areas beyond his competence. He is trained to refer clients, when necessary, to other specialists. Even counselors possessing advanced degrees seldom view their training as complete. They continue to learn and to improve their skills and services.

What Are Some of the Current Issues in Counseling?

Over the years, counselors have dealt with many issues in state, regional, and national conventions, informal meetings, and training programs. New issues constantly emerge, and old ones re-emerge to be argued, defended, or attacked. Some current issues of concern to counseling practitioners are described here.

A major issue for many counseling practitioners is the proper use of small group experiences. While the term *small group experience* covers a variety of activities—group guidance, encounter groups, marathon groups, group psychotherapy—what is at issue are the leader's qualifications or training and ethical safeguards extended to group participants. Excluding group guidance classes, where the usual emphasis is on providing educational and vocational information to groups of 20 or 30, relatively few counselors trained prior to 1965 have had much systematic preparation for conducting small group experiences.

The popularity of small group experiences among many segments of the population has grown enormously during the past several years. As in any form of counseling, adequate training to conduct such experiences is essential. In the case of group counseling, specialized training would appear mandatory. As a minimum, this should include courses in group theory and dynamics, personal participation in groups, and supervised group practicum experience.

Ethical safeguards for participants are in some ways identical with the ethics of individual counseling, but they also involve unique elements. Assuming that the leader is qualified, questions still remain about such matters as screening and follow-up counseling of participants, maintenance of confidentiality, restrictions on participants' behavior, and clients' consent to participate as well as freedom to withdraw. Undoubtedly, other ethical concerns could be identified.

Still another issue in conducting group experiences relates to the appropriateness of the activity to the goals of the setting with which the counselor is associated. Group participation has many attractive and desirable characteristics. However, common sense indicates that there are limits on the types of groups that can appropriately be conducted in certain types of settings. For example, there would seem to be little question that small group activities which focus on specific educational problems such as underachievement, career choice, or educational planning are appropriate for school counselors. Whether some schools could or would tolerate some forms of encounter groups would depend on the community and the encounter issue involved.

Currently, three observations can be noted about the use of small group experiences. First, they have received an enthusiastic reception that has sometimes led to an indiscriminate and ill-considered use of group activity. Second, the counselor must keep in mind that a relatively large percentage of the general population still has considerable fear and many reservations about group activity. Third, while there exist only a few documented cases of harm to participants, that possibility remains ever-present.

Another current issue is the degree to which the counselor should actively participate in social change or attempt to instigate change. There is no question that the counselor must be aware of the forces at work and the changes in society; yet, given the traditional role of the counselor, there is considerable question as to whether he can properly participate as a social revolutionist or engage in political power struggles, no matter how worthwhile the goal. Traditionally the counselor's primary responsibility has been to work with individuals. At the same time, most practitioners have been fully aware that their effectiveness has sometimes been thwarted by environmental conditions over which they have little control.

Currently, there is much pressure on the counselor to become an agent of change or a social activist. Few would argue that the counselor's work should be confined completely to his office. However, it is essential for the counselor to recognize that if he becomes heavily involved in his professional work as an agent of change he automatically reduces the amount of time available for working directly with individuals or groups of clients.

It should be noted also that if the professional decides there is more to be gained in social activism conducted outside his office, then such a decision has implications for training and preparation. Relatively few preparation programs currently stress consultative functions and the complexities involved in environmental modification. These two areas are highly involved in social change and would demand specialized skills and personal characteristics which differ from those commonly associated with counseling.

A fourth issue is whether a counselor from the dominant society can effectively serve minority-group individuals. This issue is highly complicated and emotional. Many have reservations about the potential effectiveness of the typical white Anglo-Saxon Protestant counselor with minority-group members. Most authorities on black culture, for example, would argue that the vast majority of counselors are deficient in their knowledge of black culture, communication skills, and perhaps even the will to work effectively with black individuals. If one adds to this the fact that most minority groups face impoverished life conditions which change very slowly, the prospects for success appear even bleaker. These factors are current realities for minority groups, and it would appear essential for the counselor to take a realistic stance in relation to them. A realistic view would mean recognizing the tremendous difficulty of the task and being fully aware that counseling assistance can help reduce, but probably not totally resolve, the factors which create and perpetuate the individual's situation. Realism also would demand a firm commitment to undertake the personal, often painful changes necessary to work productively with minority-group members.

A fifth issue lies in the use of paraprofessionals or counselor-aides. The heart of the issue seems to be which responsibilities should be delegated to such individuals. The term *paraprofessional* has been used generally to denote any individual who has less than the requisite graduate training and who works under the supervision of a qualified counselor. The educational level attained by paraprofessionals ranges from less than completion of high school to college graduation.

The counseling field could make considerable use of such individuals, especially since most counselors dislike spending time in clerical and routine tasks only marginally related to their basic function. Two observations about the issue may be noted: First, some of the adverse reactions toward the use of counselor-aides may come from counselors who are afraid they will be replaced by support personnel. Some counselors reason that support personnel cost less money than professional counselors and that once their administrators observe what counselor-aides are able to accomplish, their own counseling positions will be eliminated. The second observation is that years of experience may be needed in order to know how to employ counselor-aides wisely and appropriately. At present, counselor-aides serve mostly in peripheral functions in inner-city schools, employment counseling, and government-supported community training programs. In this capacity they often meet and work with clients before the counselor does. It is not known whether this is the case in all settings and institutions where counseling is offered. In some situations counselor-aides may be more profitably employed to work with clients after the counselor's initial and continuing intervention. Certainly in the future support personnel will be involved in both direct and indirect helping relationships. Appropriate use of counselor-aides will facilitate and extend the work of the counselor and make his task more effective.

A sixth issue revolves around the counselor's function in legal and ethical conflict situations between the individual and the institution. Should the counselor champion the individual, or give his primary loyalty to the institution? It should be noted that only rarely does a situation arise in which the counselor's responsibilities conflict this way. Usually, when the counselor is helping the individual he is also helping the institution.

Confidentiality is essential in a counseling relationship. If the counselor cannot provide this for his client, his effectiveness is severely limited. In most instances, if the counselor breaks the client's confidence, it is usually because he is convinced that to remain silent would have a disastrously harmful effect on the client or on society at large. Perhaps the basic problem for the counselor is to determine what constitutes the circumstances of such a disaster. The usual justification—probable harm to self or to others—require fairly simple decisions for most counselors. Beyond that there are, of course, no easy solutions. Each situation must be considered on its own merits, each decision must be based on the client's welfare, and pertinent parts of the profession's ethical codes must be considered.

What Are Some of the Current Trends in Counseling?

The field of counseling is undergoing fairly rapid change. New trends and directions emerge that represent special challenges and opportunities for those within it. As each new development takes place, it is carefully examined and evaluated by the practicing counselor. Some of the trends are described here so that the reader may have a better understanding of the current movements and ideas in counseling.

1. *The work of the counselor is no longer restricted to activities that take place within his office.* Originally, the counselor's work was confined primarily to providing assistance to persons who came to his office either voluntarily or through referral. One result of this practice was that only a relatively narrow range of clients received assistance. For example, individuals who sought help from the counselor in the school setting were usually college-bound students. In community clinics, clients generally were referred by professionals in allied fields.

The contemporary counselor has begun to expand his traditional role. New activities conducted outside the counselor's office have been proposed. These are designed to seek out and serve a much broader range of clientele. Not only have the types of client changed, but the counselor's activities now include more variety: consultative activities have increased, and a more vigorous interventionist approach has been adopted, aiming to modify known sources of problems among a broader population. For example, counselors in many settings are performing an educational function that might include teaching mini-courses on job application, drug abuse, sex education, military obligations, and the like. Moreover, many counselors are engaging in laboratory training in human relations and are taking a more active part in providing coordination between community agencies.

2. *The comprehensive mental health movement, beginning with federal legislation in the early to mid-1960's, has greatly*

influenced the care and treatment available to clients. The movement stresses increased reliance on locally provided services. Heavy emphasis is placed on outpatient care, minimal hospitalization, and educational and consultative services stressing preventive approaches. The need for personnel in this area has greatly broadened the range of professionals who work in comprehensive centers.

3. *Specialization continues in the counseling field.* Many individuals seek training and preparation which focuses on a subgroup within the population or on specific kinds of problems within a population. Originally the counselor tended to specialize in broad categories such as personal-social versus educational-vocational counseling. More recently there has been a proliferation of specialized services; counseling services are now available in the areas of, for instance, vocational choice, alcoholism, drugs, the draft, and abortion.

Many professionals decry such fragmentation within the field, arguing that counseling should deal with more general problems. On the other hand, in a complex society specialization seems inevitable if clients are to receive direct and useful services at critical points in their lives. Added to this is the fact that many individuals with certain kinds of problems (for example, alcoholics and drug users) distrust professional help and prefer assistance from one who has experienced the same type of problem, even if he lacks extensive professional training. This situation has led the American Board on Counseling Services to broaden its functions of evaluation, certification, and publication of a directory of approved agencies. The Board, which was created by the American Personnel and Guidance Association to evaluate agencies and individuals offering counseling services, now seeks to include those who formerly could not be certified because of a lack of credentials, professional education, treatment practices, and administrative procedures.

It seems likely that specialization will continue to develop because of (1) the increased public demand for services, (2) the individual counselor's preference for working with certain types of clients, and (3) the demand by some clients for highly focused kinds of assistance.

4. *Intensive group experiences will continue to be used in all settings that provide counseling services.* Despite the

many problems surrounding the use of intensive group experiences, group counseling and other forms of group experiences continue to be popular and sought after for a variety of reasons. Carl R. Rogers, a noted psychotherapist, has pointed out that intensive group experiences serve to alleviate voids in contemporary life often attributed to alienation, depersonalization, and lack of community. While the young seem to suffer more intensely from these negative attributes of society, loneliness permeates all age levels and will continue to account for an increased demand for group experiences. While the group experience should not be viewed as a solution for all of society's ills, its continued use will lead to an improved application of counseling for specific situations.

5. *Technology will be applied increasingly to the work of the counselor.* While this trend is sometimes viewed as contradictory to the personal relationship aspects inherent in counseling, the application of technology might preferably be viewed as a means of freeing the counselor to serve his clientele. In the area of educational and vocational information alone, there is little doubt that great use can be made of computers and other multimedia approaches to free the counselor from using valuable time in transmitting information verbally to his client. While many view these technological advances as threatening to depersonalize counseling, this will occur only if counselors allow it to happen by failing to adapt technology to their work in ways beneficial to their clients.

Some of the benefits of technology have already been employed in counselor preparation through the use of audio-video taped devices. These have enriched training by providing a broad range of demonstrations of approaches to counseling and by permitting counselors-in-training to observe and to analyze their own progress. It seems safe to predict that the application of technology to counseling services will increase in the future.

CAREER COUNSELING OPPORTUNITIES IN EDUCATIONAL SETTINGS

CHAPTER 3

This chapter seeks to describe career counseling opportunities in various educational settings, which account for the greatest number of counselors presently employed in the United States. These settings range from elementary schools through universities and include junior colleges and technical institutes. Both public and private or parochial educational institutions are involved.

Elementary Schools

The past decade has marked the emergence and rapid increase of counselors employed in elementary schools. Many individuals would argue that having counselors at the elementary school level is the most logical and critical educational level because of the need for early treatment and prevention of problems arising at this age.

Surveys of elementary school counselors within the 50 states based on data obtained in 1967 and 1968 reveal dramatically accelerating opportunities for employment. It was estimated in 1967 that approximately 3,800 counselors were employed in elementary schools. By 1968, 6,000 counselors were found in elementary schools (kindergarten through sixth grade). Approximately two-thirds were employed full time in both survey years. However, researchers who have conducted such surveys have pointed out that the term *counselor* is often applied to any specialist who works in the elementary school, regardless of what he does (psychologist, psychometrist, special education teacher, hearing and speech specialist, etc.).

During the latter part of the 1960's elementary school counseling programs received great impetus from federal monies available for such service. Many programs were supported fully or partially by federal funds. In some school districts, once these federal funds were withdrawn counselors were released from their assignments. In most of these situations, elementary school counselors were released not because of their work as counselors but because of the severe financial restrictions experienced by the school. In these districts elementary school counselors had been the last employed and were therefore the first to be released.

NATURE OF THE ELEMENTARY SCHOOL COUNSELOR'S WORK

Few teachers, school administrators, or parents question the need for elementary school counselors. The pervasive hope is that through the early identification, treatment, and prevention of problems, pupil behavioral disorders will be less serious and more temporary. It is recognized, furthermore, that early treatment might facilitate the development of a child's sense of responsibility, his decision-making skills, and his personal development. The few educators who question the need for elementary school counselors often do so on the basis that teachers are close to pupils and that children in kindergarten through sixth grade do not have to make educational or vocational choices. Presumably their rather narrow view of the purpose of counseling is to help individuals in making educational and vocational choices.

Many counselor-educators and elementary school counselors assert that elementary school counseling is different from secondary school counseling. But, when pressed to describe the differences, the usual explanation is that elementary school counselors do more counseling than the typical secondary school counselor. However, the differences between elementary and secondary school counseling have yet to be clearly set forth. Perhaps time and experience are needed in order for elementary school counseling to create an identity of its own.

For some reason—perhaps because of the closer teacher-pupil relationship—the recommended counselor-student ratio in elementary schools has tended to be two or three times greater than that of secondary schools. For many years the ratio was 600–1,000 elementary school pupils to one full-time counselor. During the past five years, however, this figure has been scaled down, and most authorities now assert that the proper ratio should be one full-time counselor for 250–300 pupils.

Elementary school counselors, like their secondary school counterparts, engage in (1) counseling individuals and small groups (six to eight pupils); (2) consulting with teachers, parents, and administrators as a resource person with special skills and knowledge; and (3) performing supporting guidance services such as testing, working with teachers on the use of vocational guidance materials with pupils, referring pupils who need special help, and conducting parent study groups. Most counselor-educators involved in preparing elementary school counselors emphasize the importance of the counseling and consultant functions, giving each more or less equal weight. Some counselors emphasize one function to the exclusion of the other. It should be recognized that the nature of counseling services in many schools places at least equal emphasis on services that support counseling, such as appraisal and informational services.

An idea of the elementary school counselor's work can be gained by scanning a summary description of a day's activities for one counselor. The following description has been provided by Mrs. Lorean Roberts, a counselor at Monnett Elementary School in Rensselaer, Indiana. The school has an enrollment of 300 students in grades 1 through 5.

A Typical Day as an Elementary School Counselor

7:45–8:15 Coffee in the teachers' lounge with most of the fifteen teachers in the school. The special education teacher and principal are usually present also. This is an opportunity to talk to the faculty, get better acquainted, and also to hear what is happening around the school. This is both an enjoyable time and a valuable time for making casual contacts.

8:15–8:30 Look over the schedule for the day. Note that a fourth-grade teacher has requested that I go to her room to lead a group discussion concerning getting along with others because of some difficulties her class has had on the playground.

8:30–9:00 A fifth-grade boy arrives for his appointment. He is new in the school. His teacher referred him because of the difficulty he was having adjusting to the new school setting, both socially and academically. He feels that the students shun him and that the teacher expects more of him than he is able to give. His mother is very protective and accompanies him to school every day.

9:00–9:30 Two first-grade girls, self-referrals, have an appointment. They want to talk about school—how it has and has not met their expectations—and about how to get people to like them and play with them on the playground.

9:30–10:00 Three boys from the third grade come in. They were referred a couple of weeks ago by their teacher. They are disruptive in the classroom and disrespectful toward their teacher, she reports. They all have been retained once. They feel left out, friendless, and think the work is too hard in third grade. After about fifteen minutes of talking about themselves, they begin to get restless and engage in horseplay. This has been their usual pattern. About five minutes before their appointment time is up, they return to a more serious mood and talk about their next appointment.

10:00–10:15 Coffee with the principal. A sort of "how has your day been so far" time. Today we talk about some of the preparations that are being made for the ungraded primary section that will be initiated next year. We set aside two days next week to finalize some plans and programs for his presentation to the school board.

10:15–11:00 A first-grade teacher is concerned about a child in her class. He has been displaying some unusual behavior that she does not understand. She has suggested that this would be a good time to observe him in the classroom, as they will be engaged in a variety of situations: study, discussion, and free time. On the way to the classroom I am stopped by the school secretary who has a message that I am to call a parent about making an appointment, and the school nurse who would like to talk to me about a student who has been in several days in a row complaining of an upset stomach and a headache. The nurse and I agree that lunchtime will probably fit our schedules best.

11:00–11:20 Time to get organized again. There are several telephone calls to make, and the fourth-grade discussion coming up needs some more thought.

11:20–11:40 Group discussion in one of the fourth grades. Some open-ended situations are presented, and students speculate about possible outcomes. This leads to talk among the students about how they feel when certain situations arise. The students decide they need to make up some fair rules for their grade to use on the playground. They choose a committee of two boys and two girls to work with the teacher on the rules. They debate about the merits of having two sets of rules, one for boys and one for girls.

11:40–12:00 This time is spent in the hall with students who are waiting to be served lunch and with some who have finished eating. (The school has a separate lunch time for grades 1 and 2, and for grades 3 through 5. The first two grades eat lunch from 11:30 to 12 and are on the playground from 12 to 12:25; the upper grades eat from 11:40 to 12:20 and have noon recess from 12:20 until 12:50.)

12:00–12:25 The school nurse and I take our lunches to her office to talk about the fourth-grade girl who has been appearing in her office every morning for several days. We decide to contact the mother (a divorcee) to see what she may be able to tell us about the situation.

12:30–1:00 A second-grade boy comes for his appointment. He has been in twice before. He appears nervous, but he is quite verbal. He wants to talk about school and himself. His teacher is his aunt, and he feels that he can't talk to anyone about things. If he talks about home, his aunt tells his mother what he says; and if he talks about school to his parents, they check it out with the relative-teacher. He just wants to talk about things in general.

1:00–1:30 A fifth-grade girl comes to the office. She is a self-referral, as was the second-grade boy who was here the last half-hour. She needs to earn some money and does not know how to get it. She is afraid to ask her mother to let her baby-sit, because she complains when she has to take care of her little brother. She doesn't think her parents will let her do housework or ironing for other people unless she does the same things at home first. She realizes that there are very few things she can do to earn money at her age.

1:30–2:15 Work on a report on the testing program in the school. This report covers three years of standardized testing and has been compiled in such a way to show trends within the school, within grades, and within particular classes as they progressed through three grades. It appears that it will be valuable in curriculum planning, especially in the area of language arts.

2:15–2:55 A second-grade student who has been referred by his teacher arrives. There has been some question about placement of this boy. The teacher has reason to believe that he may need to be transferred to the special education class. After talking to her about her observations and reasons for thinking this, I had suggested we do some more observing and that a short mental-abilities test be administered prior to referral to the school psychologist. He is here now for the test.

2:55–3:15 This time is reserved to be used as necessary as situations arise during the day. School is dismissed at 3:15. Some days it is used for talking with teachers, some days for seeing students who cannot wait for an appointment at a later date. It seems to be a convenient time for parents to come in to see me. On other days it may be used as a preparation time for some classroom guidance materials. Today the speech therapist has come in to talk about a kindergarten student she has been working with. She would like to have me come to the kindergarten soon and observe her working with the child. She has some ideas about what may be causing the child's difficulties, but would like to clarify her thinking by talking things over with another person who has observed the child.

3:15–4:00 The library is next-door to my office. The librarian comes in to vent a few hostile feelings and to get some ideas about what she can do with a couple of classes she is having difficulty handling. She is also having trouble dealing with some teachers and wants to talk about the pressures she is feeling from several sources. While we are talking, the

> teacher of the first student I saw this morning comes into the office and wants to know what went on in the conference with his student. This situation arises frequently and is a difficult topic to broach and still maintain a good teacher-counselor relationship. The three of us go to the teachers' lounge before leaving school just to see what is going on in there.

Considerable debate has taken place as to whether counseling or consulting is the major function in the elementary school counselor's work. Persons who feel that the elementary school counselor should function primarily as a consultant claim the child will be helped best when teachers, parents, and principals change their behavior in order to create a better environment for him and others and when they become better informed about the child and his behavior.

Cecil H. Patterson, a psychologist at the University of Illinois, questions the desirability of having the elementary school counselor devote full time to consultant activities. He believes that if the counselor becomes "nothing but a consultant," he becomes remote from and uninvolved with children—with the result that the counselor's observations become evaluative and his viewpoint external. Patterson charges that it is ". . . those who are not closely involved in schools or with children, including some counselor educators and U.S. Office of Education officials, who would deemphasize counseling and replace it by consulting or coordinating functions." In practice, most elementary schools want to employ a counselor who does both. The two functions are complementary: One focuses directly on children, the other indirectly helps an individual through working with others who are important to him.

Elementary school counseling programs which were launched with the support of federal or state funds usually were located in a single school building (housing kindergarten through sixth grade). However, some programs have been initiated with a full-time counselor serving more than one building in a school district.

DEMAND FOR ELEMENTARY SCHOOL COUNSELORS

The demand for elementary school counselors has exceeded the supply since 1964, when the National Defense Education

Act was amended to permit state education departments to extend financial support to counseling programs in elementary schools. Further amendments in 1968, and later the Education Professions Development legislation, authorized training programs to prepare counselors for elementary schools.

The demand for elementary school counselors is not likely to decrease. In 1967, approximately 6,000 counselors were working in elementary schools; but given the elementary school enrollment, more than 88,000 would have been required to meet the recommended ratio of 1: 300. Further, in 1970–1971 about 90,000 counselors were needed to meet this recommended ratio.

PREPARATION REQUIRED

Preparation of elementary school counselors takes place at the graduate level. Currently, most counselors have had one year of counselor preparation plus additional graduate courses. Universities which train elementary school counselors usually require coursework in child development and psychology, an introductory course in elementary school guidance, a counseling practicum with elementary school children, and a course in consulting. These courses are additional to the coursework required of all counselors such as statistics, mental measurement, counseling theory, and group processes. More and more state departments of education are establishing certification requirements for elementary school counselors. In many states the standards for certifying or endorsing elementary school counselors differ little, if any, from those for secondary school counselors.

WORKING CONDITIONS

Working conditions vary greatly in elementary schools where counselors are employed. During the late 1960's counselors were often assigned to two or more schools, many of which were in the inner city. Few elementary schools have been constructed with counseling facilities. The physical facilities for counseling were often primitive and provided little privacy. Many schools modified classrooms or cloakrooms in order to provide an area for counseling. However, federal, state, and local funds often made it possible for the elementary school counselor to purchase tape recorders, play media, and other necessary equipment.

SALARIES

Few differences exist between the pay scale for secondary and elementary school counselors. Most school personnel are employed on a schedule that rewards training and experience. The average elementary school counselor's salary in 1971 was $8,500.

CURRENT ISSUES

Reference has been made to the issue of whether the elementary school counselor is primarily a counselor or a consultant. Another major issue is his use of play media (puppets, dolls, clay, drawings, etc.). Essentially the issue is whether the counselor's use of such media is primarily to establish a good working relationship with the child or whether the products produced by the child from such media are to be used by the counselor to interpret and treat the child's behavior. There is no question that a child's attitudes, motives, and imagination, closely associated with his life situation and actual experiences, are reflected in his play. Play therapy is based on encouraging the child to re-enact situations in which he has emotional difficulty, so that he can display feelings which are inhibited in the real situation. Therefore play therapy, in our view, remains a specialized technique of the child psychologist and psychiatrist. This does not mean that elementary school counselors should not use play media to put a child at ease or to establish a relationship with him or even to understand his behaviors (that is, to talk with the child about his play and its possible meanings). Play therapy, however, is a special treatment procedure which should be engaged in only by persons with clinical training and supervised experience.

Another important issue is whether the elementary school counselor possesses the skills to administer individual intelligence tests. Some preparation programs require that elementary school counselors be equipped to do so. Professors in these programs argue that, since most schools do not have the services of school psychometrists or school psychologists, elementary school counselors are the logical persons to conduct intellectual assessments of children. Others who oppose this undertaking by counselors assert that psychometrists should be employed by schools and that counselors should confine their work to counseling and consulting. Undoubtedly, counselors who have received such training in their preparation programs will spend much of their time in individual testing. In such cases, they are practicing psychometry, not counseling, and their titles should be changed to reflect their functions.

It should be noted that the same issue arises if an elementary school counselor has extensive training in other specialty areas, such as remedial reading or speech therapy. While it is true that such preparation can be helpful in the counselor's work, it should be kept in mind that if the individual enters the school as a counselor, then his primary work responsibility is in that field despite the pressing need for other special services.

CAREER PATTERNS

Most contemporary elementary school counselors have had experience as teachers. The usual career pattern is to teach for two or more years, undergo preparation as a counselor, and then find employment as an elementary school counselor. Many elementary school teachers are women. Prior to the emergence of elementary school counseling, their career alternatives were either to become an elementary school principal, to seek preparation and then enter special education programs, or to remain a classroom teacher. Counseling opens a new career avenue for them, and many capable individuals have pursued that opportunity.

OUTLOOK

The outlook for elementary school counselors appears promising. Despite some cutback in elementary school counseling positions during 1970 and 1971, it is anticipated that a healthier economy will bring increased employment of elementary school counselors.

SOURCES OF FURTHER INFORMATION

An important source of information about elementary school counseling is *Elementary School Guidance and Counseling*, a journal issued four times a year by the American Personnel and Guidance Association (APGA). The APGA and its division, the American School Counselor Association (ASCA), have published materials which are helpful and informative for one who plans an elementary school counseling career. Many elementary school counselors are members of ASCA and APGA.

Secondary Schools

The public secondary school is the setting in which counseling has experienced tremendous development. Currently it is estimated that some 40,000 counselors are employed in secondary schools. Several reasons have been cited to account for the employment of counselors at this educational level. These include:

the vast number of students served by the school, who are characterized by a diversity of ability, aspirations, and antecedent experiences;

the diversity in curriculum offerings and the educational choices and planning that must be made if students are to pursue relevant educational experiences;

state and federal subsidies for the development of counseling and testing programs;

recognition that a loss of talent might be counteracted by employing counselors who would help students in such problem areas as underachievement, leaving school early, lack of motivation, drugs, educational deficits, adapting to changing social and economic conditions;

a growing public concern that each student's personal development should be facilitated.

Secondary school counselors are not expected to act as judges or evaluators. They differ from teachers and administrators as well as parents in this respect. They are not responsible directly, as are teachers, for seeing that students meet or exceed standards of subject matter achievement. Consequently, counselors can establish relationships free from threat and unrestricted in scope—relationships that will facilitate individual growth and development. Counselors exist at this level of education to aid students in understanding the variety, depth, and breadth of their personal experiences, the opportunities available to them, and the choices open to them. Students are helped to recognize, interpret, and act upon their personal strengths and resources.

NATURE OF THE SECONDARY SCHOOL COUNSELOR'S WORK

The nature of counseling practice in secondary schools has changed over time, slowly but perceptibly. Traditionally their practice involved serving as a quasi-administrator or "handyman" who took disciplinary action, administered schoolwide tests, conducted extracurricular activities, sponsored student government councils, assigned teachers and students to classes, and occasionally managed to interview a few students. Until 1960 this description was frequently encountered when counselors were asked what activities occupied their time. It stressed little counseling contact with students, but rather emphasized efficient administrative management of the student body. Although vestiges of this outmoded concept of counselor practice remain, a marked change has taken place in the functions of counselors since 1960. The change was due to many factors of which the most important was the requirement of a counseling practicum (supervised counseling experience with clients) in the entry-level preparation of counselors.

Today, the secondary school counselor specializes in the helping relationship. He gives priority to individual and group counseling. While counseling occupies most of his time, the secondary school counselor also engages in (1) consulting with teachers, administrators, and others, and (2) conducting supporting counseling functions such as maintaining occupational information files, testing, etc. As a specialist in the helping relationship, then, the nature of the counselor's work involves the following services:

1. *Counseling.* He counsels students on an individual and small-group basis in such matters as educational and vocational choices and planning, understanding their own and others' behavior, developing a sense of identity, coping with stressful situational and emotional conflicts, making decisions, and getting along with others.

2. *Consulting.* He consults with teachers, administrators, and parents about students and the school environment. The counselor works closely with teachers and shares their understanding of students' behaviors and needs as exhibited in the classroom, with due regard to the confidentiality of the data so that teachers may serve students better. He helps teachers

identify students who have special needs or problems requiring special attention. He works with administrators regarding characteristics of the student body and possible modification of the school environment. He consults with parents to help them understand their children better and to inform them of the opportunities and services available to them.

3. *Student appraisal.* He coordinates the accumulation of test and non-test student appraisal data in the areas of achievement, ability, personality, and interest. He interprets these data to students, teachers, parents, and others who need to know.

4. *Educational and vocational planning and placement.* The counselor provides students with information about future educational and vocational opportunities and requirements.

5. *Referral work.* The counselor makes referrals to other school specialists (speech and hearing therapists, social workers, psychologists) and to specialists in public and private community agencies.

Perhaps some understanding of the nature of counseling in a secondary school may be obtained by inspecting a counselor's activities on a typical day. The following time schedule has been supplied by Mrs. Alice Arthur, a counselor at West Lafayette Senior High School, West Lafayette, Indiana. Her daily appointments and recollections—omitting some minor interruptions of her schedule—are more or less as follows.

A Typical Day as a Secondary School Counselor

Office open 8:00–4:30; classes in session 8:15–3:15; month of February

8:00–8:20	Scan daily appointments. Telephone call from parent about absent student. Review announcement preparation (for 10:15 announcements). Take care of emergency problems, i.e. "coming to school incidents," teacher requests, etc.
8:20–9:00	Contact students who are to be seen this week concerning fall schedules (average six per hour in conference room setting).

9:00–9:15	Short conference with principal concerning plans to counsel with a student who has been in poor attendance. Principal will take care of disciplinary measures, if necessary, but counselor hopes to work with helping individual understand the cause of the problem through a series of counseling sessions.
9:15–10:15	See six students on our regular planned scheduling interview for fall scheduling. They are from the same grade level (sophomore), and will be coming from study hall. They will be seen together, but each schedule will be reviewed individually with the student, then taken home for parent approval.
10:15–10:30	Morning announcements given by the principal—important to listen to know what activities and concerns involve students and staff. Some students come in asking for SAT registration forms, class rank information, scholarship information, etc. Introduced college representative to two prospective students who have indicated an interest in the given college. Counselor will receive literature, but time does not allow attendance at every representative's presentation.
10:30–11:00	Prepare for afternoon appointment with parents concerning achievement and future program for ninth grader. Collect records, review teacher information forms which were sent out when appointment was made, request secretary to compile most recent six-week grades. Answer telephone calls.
11:00–11:20	Confer with counseling staff about planned sophomore testing program set for March. Responsibilities assigned, etc.
11:20–12:15	Scheduled appointment with eleventh-grade girl. She had made the statement: "I see other people's choice of college and career 'just happening'—but I want to do some planning, yet I have no ideas. Can you help me?" This is the first of several meetings we have planned to explore career and college for her.
12:20–12:40	Lunch in cafeteria.
12:40–1:15	To teacher's lounge to socialize and to see teachers concerning: (a) A student who had been absent and fell be-

hind in his work now fears return to class—is teacher aware of tension?
(b) Placement of a student in proper math class for fall.
(c) Item of business on Student-Faculty Committee agenda.

1:15–1:30 Review afternoon appointments. Answer telephone calls.

1:30–2:30 Conference with parents of ninth grader (see 10:30 item). Ask secretary to hold calls during conference.

2:30–3:15 Students arrive for scheduling conference—both counselors work together and complete 15 student schedules.

3:15–3:30 Drop-in time—students with variety of small questions.

3:30–4:00 Dictate to secretary concerning:
(a) Special materials needed for fall program for blind student counselee.
(b) Memo on parent conference for counselor's folder.
(c) Notes on teacher conferences at noon.
(d) Receive day's college applications for signing (secretary does form work; counselor's statement is written by counselor then typed by secretary).

4:15–4:30 Straighten desk, set priorities for next day.

PREPARATION REQUIRED

As in the case of virtually any educational job, entry into secondary school counseling positions requires state certification. Almost all states and territories specify that counselors must have completed 15 to 30 hours and/or hold a master's degree comprised of graduate counseling courses. Some states have a two- or three-step plan in their counselor certification program. Step 1, which is often provisional, may require the applicant to have from six to 12 hours of graduate credit; step 2 requires the individual to have completed 12 to 24 hours; and step 3 often requires 24 to 40 hours or more, or a specialist degree or certificate. The steps apply only to persons already holding a bachelor's degree, and in most cases teacher certification is a prerequisite.

At present, most states require from one to five years of teaching experience for permanent school counselor certification. While the teaching experience requirement is slowly being changed (approximately five states do not require it or are experimenting with dropping the requirement), it will be some time before the requirement is abolished nationally.

Most universities with counselor preparation programs have certain requirements that candidates must meet before they can be recommended for state certification or employment. These requirements are often additional to those of the state departments of education. For example, many current counselor preparation programs will not recommend candidates who have not taken the supervised individual and group counseling practicum, which too often is listed as an optional requirement by state standards. Further information about courses required for a degree in school counseling may be found in Chapter 2. Persons interested in secondary school counseling should contact the department of education in the state in which they seek employment, since requirements do vary from state to state.

Counselor education programs are available in about 400 colleges and universities primarily within departments of education or psychology. To obtain a master's degree a student must, in most instances, complete one to two years of graduate work.

WORKING CONDITIONS

Since World War II, most communities and cities have built new junior and senior high schools or have extensively remodeled old facilities. While not all communities provide the ideal facilities for counseling, many have designed physical facilities which provide comfort and privacy for the counselor's work. The major problems of secondary school counselors in regard to satisfactory working conditions has usually been to secure adequate secretarial and clerical assistance, as well as to obtain sufficient time and the administrative approval for engaging in personal-social counseling.

SALARIES

As for elementary school counselors, salaries for secondary school counselors are determined by the salary schedule of the particular school system. The American School Counselors Association, based on a 20 percent sample of its membership, reported that in 1970 the mean salary for male counselors was $9,000, while that of female counselors was

$8,000. Approximately two-thirds of the sample reported that they were on a 10-month, or less, salary schedule. During the past decade, when counselors were in short supply, many school districts paid counselors additional increments (from approximately $100 to $1,000) above salary schedule figures. Such increments were given usually if counselors worked evenings or during the summer. A few districts offered more money because of the need to attract and hold qualified personnel.

CURRENT ISSUES

A seemingly ever-present issue is whether teaching experience should be required for entry into school counseling. Persons who advocate this requirement claim that the experience (1) enables counselors to be accepted more readily by teachers; (2) helps counselors to understand the school and classroom problems; (3) serves as a period of time for individuals to mature and to decide whether they want to pursue graduate work in the field; and (4) helps confirm that counselors are committed to a career in the field of education. Persons who are opposed to requiring teaching experience often assert that (1) what is learned in teaching does not necessarily apply to counseling; (2) acceptance by teachers is based more on the individual's personal characteristics and capabilities than on his previous job activities; (3) opening school counseling to other disciplines provides a better source of supply for able candidates; and (4) such a requirement lengthens unduly the preservice time required for individuals to be able to practice as counselors.

While arguments over this issue continue, the American School Counselor Association has proposed and adopted the resolution that teaching experience ought not to be the only route available for an individual to become a secondary school counselor. However, the issue will undoubtedly be discussed until state departments of education remove teaching experience as a requirement for counselor certification.

Another issue currently receiving much attention is the relevance of membership in the American Personnel and Guidance Association for secondary school counselors. The APGA, founded in 1951–1952, is an association comprised of several organizations concerned with counseling, guidance, and student personnel work. There are now eight divisions within the APGA structure.

The American School Counselor Association, APGA's main counseling division, contains the largest group of APGA members (approximately 12,000 of the 27,000 members). Some ASCA members and officers have contended that (1) APGA leadership and the central office staff have been inattentive to the needs of counselor members in the association, and (2) ASCA, given its membership and resources, does not have its proper share of influence within the APGA structure. Consequently, these members have urged that the association disaffiliate from APGA and that school counselors either establish their own organization or affiliate with the National Education Association. A poll of ASCA members was conducted in late 1970 to ascertain whether the association should disaffiliate from APGA. Few members responded, but those who were heard from voted overwhelmingly to remain within the APGA structure. Attention is currently being given to restructuring APGA government in an attempt to provide better services to members. It is hoped that these projected modifications will enable the parent organization, as well as its divisions and state branches, to meet the practitioner's interests and needs.

CAREER PATTERNS

Traditionally, the career progression for secondary school counselors has been from teacher to counselor to principal. However, while this career pattern was representative of the field before 1960, it no longer holds true. Typical career patterns include:

1. remaining a counselor, usually moving from small or rural schools to larger, city or suburban schools;

2. serving as a counselor for one or more years and then becoming a director or supervisor of guidance or counseling. A person may remain in this capacity until retirement, perhaps making lateral career shifts into better financed school districts or pursuing vertical shifts through administering a school-wide pupil personnel program (which includes counseling, psychological services, social work, etc.);

3. serving as a school counselor for one or more years and then entering an advanced graduate preparation pro-

gram to become a college counselor, counselor-educator, educational psychologist, or school psychologist.

These three career patterns are appearing with increasing frequency, as movement from counseling into administration is no longer the only route available to or pursued by counselors. Career development in counseling, as in other occupations, occurs within a situational context as a result of interaction over time between the personality of the counselor and the demands of the employment setting.

OUTLOOK

Employment opportunities for secondary school counselors during the 1970's are expected to vary from good to excellent. However, the early 1970's has been a period in which a number of school counselors have experienced difficulty in obtaining entry-level positions. Two reasons have been mainly responsible for this difficulty. First, many school districts have suffered severe financial problems because they were at the maximum legal tax rate permitted them. Largely as a result of inflationary costs, school districts could not employ new personnel and, in some cases, had to cut back existing programs and personnel. Second, many individuals who sought entry-level counseling positions did not have teaching or counseling experience and were therefore not competitive because they lacked full certification.

Most observers believe that an alleviation of the tax problems encountered by schools will change the somewhat difficult employment situation presently experienced by entry-level school counselors. However, projections of an excess number of teachers for the 1970's may produce an ever-increasing supply of candidates for counseling training and employment.

The critical shortage of secondary school counselors which has characterized the field for several years seems now to have ended. On the other hand, job openings for counselors are expected to increase during the 1970's due to a strengthening of counseling services to reach a more realistic student-counselor ratio of one full-time counselor to approximately 250 students. Moreover, it is estimated that a 10 percent attrition rate occurs among practicing counselors, so that many counselors are required in order to replace those who leave the profession. A statement of the outlook for secondary school counseling must also take into account that there is a growing public awareness of the value of helping students with their personal, educational, and vocational problems. This public recognition is reflected in the funding provided by the federal government for secondary school counseling programs, particularly in vocational education legislation.

SOURCES OF FURTHER INFORMATION

The American Personnel and Guidance Association is a major source of information about secondary school counseling. Its main counseling division, the American School Counselor Association, has given much attention to the collection and dissemination of information about the field. Some of the publications which may be of interest to persons considering the field include:

Meet Your Secondary School Counselor, leaflet, free copy available.

What to Expect from School Counselors, a 28-page public affairs pamphlet, No. 402, one to nine copies at 25 cents each.

The Role of the Secondary School Counselor, a condensed statement based on "Statement of Policy for Secondary School Counselors" and "Guidelines for Implementation" approved by the membership and adopted by the Governing Board of ASCA, 1964. Free copy available.

Vocational and Technical Schools

Although the history of vocational education stretches back to early colonial times, 1917 marks the first year of support from the federal government. It is only recently, in the United States, that as much attention has been given to vocational education as to preparation for college.

In its broadest sense, *vocational education* includes any experiences or activities designed to aid students to become more efficient in vocational pursuits. More narrowly defined, vocational education is viewed as preparation for a particular occupation, except for professional occupations or those requiring a baccalaureate degree.

Clearly, the scope of modern vocational education is very broad. Its program possibilities are almost infinite, and its potential as an educational force is just now beginning to be developed. It is estimated that 14 million students will be enrolled in vocational and technical education programs by 1975. Despite this projection, many persons retain the attitude that vocational education consists of inferior programs for inferior students and that only traditional college preparation has prestige. Yet college preparation has little meaning or reality for thousands of young people who have no desire for it or who lack the motivation or background to engage in it. The high school boy or girl who prepares for a job instead of college often loses prestige in the eyes of his teachers and friends. However, these attitudes are changing, albeit slowly, and vocational education is moving away from its inferior status.

At one time, vocational and technical education institutions, compared to secondary schools, served a relatively narrow spectrum of individuals. This is no longer the case. Currently these institutions are meeting the needs of people who vary widely in ability, age, and educational background. Individuals served by vocational and technical education programs include students who leave or graduate from high school without a marketable skill, unemployed or underemployed adults, workers whose skills or knowledge must be increased or updated, older workers whose work skills are no longer marketable, apprentices in skilled trades and technical occupations, foremen and supervisors who need leadership training, workers with physical and emotional handicaps, and persons handicapped by impoverished backgrounds.

The fundamental purpose of vocational education is to enable individuals to enter and maintain themselves in useful, gainful employment. This means more than the acquisition of skills or technical competence required for entry-level jobs; it includes a mastery of technical, social, adaptive, and conceptual skills that will enable the individual to profit from on-the-job learning and to grow and mature as a worker and as a person.

Some of the areas of preparation in vocational education programs include:

1. *Agricultural education.* Instruction is provided in growing foods and fibers, producing farm supplies, developing farm services, and processing farm products for consump-

tion. Horticulture, forestry, and conservation courses are usually available.

2. *Business and office education.* A wide variety of management, secretarial, clerical, accounting, and data-processing skills are taught.

3. *Distributive education.* Preparation in distribution, marketing, and sales occupations found in retail, wholesale, finance, insurance, real estate, transportation, utilities, and communications organizations.

4. *Home economics education.* Preparation for responsibilities in the home and for entering occupations that use home economics knowledge and skills.

5. *Trade and industrial education.* Programs in this area are designed to develop the skills and technical knowledge essential for initial employment and for advancement in a wide range of semi-skilled, skilled, and technical occupations.

6. *Technical education.* Technical education is concerned with design, development, testing, and supervisory functions.

7. *Community service programs.* Training is given in the duties, procedures, and techniques of law enforcement, fire fighting, and emergency and rescue services.

Vocational and technical education is packaged and offered in a variety of secondary and post-secondary school institutions: comprehensive high schools, area vocational schools, residential vocational centers, separate vocational (often called polytechnical) high schools, technical institutes, two-year colleges, skill centers, and sheltered workshops. New schools are being built each year. Some training programs are six weeks or less in length; others, two years or more.

Technical institutes offer education and training for occupations in which the worker depends largely on technical information and the laws of science, mathematics, and technology to accomplish his task. Two-year post-high school programs are designed to prepare technicians to support professionals in engineering, mental and physical health services, science, public service, office, agriculture, and distribution occupations. Students are prepared to work in a team relationship with professionals and associates at highly skilled levels of employment.

NATURE OF THE VOCATIONAL COUNSELOR'S WORK

The U.S. Office of Education has estimated that about 1,000 counselors were employed in 1970 in the various institutions offering vocational and technical education. This figure is expected to increase to 1,200 by 1975.

Obviously the vocational counselor spends much of his time in educational and vocational counseling and planning with students. Perhaps not so obvious is the fact that much educational-vocational counseling and planning is bound up with emotional components. While many clients have urgent needs for information about the labor market, education and training opportunities, job requirements, worker activities, and the like, most have equally urgent needs for information about themselves, their strengths and weaknesses, their relationships with others, their values and aspirations. Thus, the nature of the vocational counselor's work is similar in many ways to that of counselors in other settings. For example, one national survey (Robert E. Campbell, *Vocational Guidance in Secondary Education,* December 1968) reported the median percent of time spent by area vocational school counselors ($N = 59$) as follows: counseling, 30 percent; orientation of students, 8 percent; conferences with parents, 5 percent; test administration, 5 percent; conferences with teachers, 5 percent; preparation of reports, 5 percent; career days, 2 percent; conferences with potential employees, 2 percent; and assisting dropouts, 3 percent. In addition, these area vocational school counselors reported that within each counseling category, 30 percent or more of the counselor's time was spent in helping students with personal and emotional problems.

The work of a vocational counselor includes helping students to select appropriate vocational curricula and to obtain post-school job placement. He works with students who experience difficulty in attaining satisfactory course performance levels and in selecting activities which are of interest to them. Most important, the vocational counselor's work includes helping high school graduates and dropouts as well as adults who seek vocational preparation to clarify and become purposeful in their career plans.

Some vocational counselors devote part of their time to supervising paraprofessionals. These support personnel have been employed in some vocational and technical institutions to collect, disseminate, and interpret occupational information, administer tests, engage in establishing and maintaining relationships with industrial and business agencies, locate employment opportunities, and serve a contact or "outreach" function with disadvantaged individuals.

Clarence W. Austin, a counselor in the Connersville Area Vocational School (Indiana), has supplied the following description of his activities in that capacity.

Services of a Vocational Counselor

Services to students

1. Participate in study and development of entrance criteria and enrollment procedures for specific curricula.
2. Provide information through various means relative to student needs.
3. Plan and prepare orientation programs for high school students.
4. Select appropriate types of ability, aptitude, and interest tests to be used in the guidance and evaluation of the student.
5. Provide individual counseling (*a*) to interpret ability, interest, and aptitude to each student and parents, and (*b*) to aid in the selection of the proper curriculum.
6. Plan assembly and group guidance sessions dealing with the world of work and its realities.
7. Scan daily classified ad sections of newspapers of area and adjacent metropolitan centers and make contact with potential employers.
8. Assist students in preparing credentials and employment applications.
9. Arrange interviews between students and prospective employers.
10. Maintain adequate and accurate cumulative records; furnish transcripts and other information from these records to prospective employers.
11. Conduct follow-up studies of students who have left the school.

Services to other school personnel

1. Conduct in-service workshops with guidance personnel in participating schools.
2. Maintain close liaison with participating school officials.

3. Conduct in-service programs to inform all teachers about the objectives and training provided.
4. Work closely and cooperatively with all vocational teachers and administrators in terms of the students' orderly and successful progress through school.
5. Participate in the identification of curricular needs.
6. Establish a representative vocational guidance committee to function as need warrants.

Services to community

1. Participate in program planning for "parents' night," etc., in local schools.
2. Maintain a close working relationship with existing public and private agencies for the purpose of job placement and other community services.
3. Establish a first-name relationship with trade associations, labor unions, contractors, personnel managers in business and industry, or other potential employers.
4. Plan and arrange for an annual business and industry visiting day in order that prospective employers may become familiar with the training activities.
5. Contact business and industry in follow-up studies of students who are employees.
6. Establish an area vocational guidance advisory committee which includes representation of the school vocational guidance committee and community leaders.
7. Assist in public dissemination of information relating to vocational education in general and especially vocational guidance.

Other service

1. Evaluate the effectiveness of the vocational guidance program.

PREPARATION REQUIRED

A program specifically designed to prepare counselors for vocational-technical educational institutions has not yet been advanced by any national organization concerned with vocational education or guidance. However, many professors in counselor education have proposed the following graduate coursework:

Introduction to guidance

Theories of and factors influencing vocational development

Use of career informational materials and resources

Counseling theory and techniques

Group processes

Counseling practicum (clients with vocational and educational problems)

Adolescent development

Statistics

Tests and measurements

History and philosophy of vocational education

Organization of and programs in vocational and technical education

Counseling internship in vocational education settings

Currently, persons who seek preparation as a vocational counselor take the usual sequence of counseling courses with additional coursework comprised of programs in graduate vocational education. A number of practicing vocational counselors have suggested that their preparation could have been improved by more seminar and supervised counseling experiences and by the use of occupational or career information, including the use of technology as applied to career information.

WORKING CONDITIONS

While some new physical facilities for vocational education have been constructed recently, particularly in area and regional vocational schools, many programs are conducted in makeshift buildings. Few institutions provide specifically designed counseling offices. In addition, the existing ratio of students to counselors appears to be higher in vocational education programs than in other educational institutions.

SALARIES

Few sources are available for estimating counselors' salaries in vocational and technical education programs. Presumably the salary level is comparable to that of counselors in secondary schools.

CURRENT ISSUES

A major issue often raised by vocational educators is the lack of previous "practical" work experience by counselors.

Some vocational educators argue that counselors know little about nonprofessional work and even less about trade and industrial workers because all of their previous experience lies in educational and professional endeavors. They question how counselors with little or no work experience and little or no contact with skilled and unskilled workers, union officials, businessmen, or industrial personnel can be of help to adolescents and adults who are not likely to enter the professional occupations. Presumably, from their point of view, a vocational counselor with direct experience in a nonprofessional occupation is best equipped for his position. While it is slowly changing, counselor certification in some states requires one or more years of employment experience outside the school setting.

Most vocational educators do not deny the value of "practical" employment experience or any experience which increases the counselor's understanding of an individual's work and his relationships with others. However, they argue against the stipulation that such experience be required before one can become a counselor. They usually agree that practical experience as a brick-layer would probably enable the counselor to be more empathetic with a person interested in brick-laying, but argue that it is not likely to be helpful in counseling a person interested in other industrial occupations. Furthermore, they point out that many if not most counselors have been employed in a variety of unskilled, semi-skilled, and skilled jobs during their undergraduate years. However, the issue remains unsettled and will no doubt continue to be raised from time to time.

Another issue in vocational education is the relevance of the individual's preparation program for his employment. It is charged that programs in vocational education preparation are outmoded and that the individual is trained for a given occupation with skills that are no longer appropriate. Those who assert this charge call not only for modernizing the program's equipment and updating the work processes, but also for preparing the individual to cope with change and to develop the capacity to acquire continually new vocational, personal, and social skills. Undoubtedly future vocational-technical education programs must somehow achieve greater flexibility in order to satisfy the needs of a diverse population.

CAREER PATTERNS

Career patterns for vocational counselors, as for school counselors, are becoming more diverse. Many vocational counselors serve as school counselors prior to their employment in vocational and technical education programs. In their undergraduate preparation some counselors specialize in vocational education, while others study in the academic areas. In many vocational education settings there is a great need for directors of pupil personnel services. A number of counselors, after a few years of experience in counseling, are likely to move into these positions.

OUTLOOK

Federal and state expenditures for vocational and technical education programs are expected to increase dramatically between 1970 and 1975. The need for counselors in these programs is urgent. Nationwide opportunities during the next few years for vocational counselors provide a bright outlook.

SOURCE OF FURTHER INFORMATION

Campbell, Robert E. *Vocational Guidance in Secondary Education: Results of a Nationwide Survey.* Columbus: Ohio State University, Center for Vocational and Technical Education, 1968. 178 pp.

Community and Junior Colleges

A movement unparalleled in educational history has taken place during the past 20 years. Although the concept that higher education should be available to the masses has been advanced as an American ideal for many years, never before has it been so enthusiastically accepted. Recently many new educational institutions—junior and community colleges, technical institutes, and college branches or regional centers—have been built to extend post-high school education to the general public. These institutions came into being primarily as a result of two converging forces: The first was the American people's expectations that higher education should be universally available and financially possible for all; the second was that established colleges and universities imposed increasingly higher admissions standards and tuition costs.

While the first two-year college (Monticello College, in Alton, Illinois) was established in 1835, the development of junior colleges occurred slowly until after World War II. At that time, the belief that every high school graduate had the right to attend college directly conflicted with the rising admissions standards of four-year colleges and universities. Moreover, the pervasive idea developed that these new two-year colleges should include a wider range of educational offerings, including programs leading to transfer to four-year colleges, technical education, community services, and remedial and developmental educational activities.

Two-year colleges appeal to students who are undecided about future careers and who are unprepared to choose a field of specialization. Such institutions provide a chance for many who may not wish to commit themselves to a four-year college career to try out higher education without great risks of time or money. In addition, they offer an opportunity for continuing education to working adults who seek to upgrade their skills and training. For these reasons, legislative enactments have been passed which enable junior and community colleges to be created and built in state after state. By 1960 it was estimated that about 600,000 students were enrolled in two-year colleges, and by 1970 enrollment had grown to almost two million students in over 1,000 two-year colleges.

No accurate single image of the two-year college can be presented. A variety of institutions are available, and several terms are used to describe them.

Junior colleges are public or private two-year colleges whose primary emphasis is on courses and programs transferable to four-year colleges.

Community colleges are comprehensive, public two-year colleges that offer post-high school preparation programs to meet the educational needs of the community, including academic or transfer programs, technical and vocational courses, general, remedial, and continuing adult education.

University extension centers or, in some cases, branch colleges provide educational services to the population that supports the parent institution.

Technical institutes provide technical preparation for individuals who expect to work at a skill level between the professional and the skilled craftsman. (These institutes were described in the previous section on vocational education.)

Two-year colleges may be privately or publicly controlled. Private junior colleges reached their peak in 1947, when they numbered 323; since then their number has declined to approximately 260. Community colleges in 1970 numbered approximately 580, of which about 70 were members of the National University Extension Association. Included in the number were about 180 two-year technical institutes, two-thirds of which were publicly controlled, and 80 four-year institutions.

NATURE OF THE TWO-YEAR COLLEGE COUNSELOR'S WORK

The work of counselors in two-year colleges is similar in many ways to that of counselors in other educational institutions. Counseling is particularly crucial for students who attend two-year colleges. Many of them have yet to establish clear educational or career goals. Some are unusually vulnerable to financial, academic, or personal pressures, or a combination of these factors.

One of the counselor's major functions is to provide assistance to students in selecting an appropriate educational program. While this activity may be viewed by some as rather routine, students who attend two-year colleges often do so under conditions not always experienced by those who attend four-year colleges. Many of these students have financial problems and must work part-time (some as much as 40 hours per week or more); others lack clearly defined educational or vocational goals; and of course, some have unrealistic educational and vocational aspirations. Furthermore, comparative studies of the characteristics of two-year college students and their counterparts in four-year colleges have frequently reported that the former (1) come from wider socioeconomic backgrounds (more lower-class students attend junior colleges), and (2) are less academically able than four-year college students. Moreover, the counselor employed in a two-year college encounters numerous students who plan to continue their education at other institutions and who need help in determining acceptable coursework which will transfer without loss of credit. Many need help not only in selecting coursework but also in selecting future institutions appropriate to their academic, vocational, and financial needs. Some research findings indicate that about two-thirds of the students in two-year colleges plan to transfer to four-year institutions but that only about one-third actually do so. Thus, counselors in two-year colleges are heavily involved in vocational and educational counseling to help students clarify and modify their goals.

Two-year college counselors engage in personal counseling. Such students are at a critical age, often attempting to achieve independence while continuing to live at home. They often experience unique and severe stress in coping with their parents' demands or attempts to regulate their lives. Often their class, study, and work schedules make it necessary for them to deviate from established family patterns, which creates additional disruption in family relationships. Thus the process of disengaging from parental control, begun in high school, continues at an intensified, accelerating rate in the two-year college. Some students, of course, fall in love and plan to marry and, because they are not really sure of themselves, seek the assistance of a counselor.

At least half of the two-year college students with whom the counselor comes into contact are adults. Most are engaged in full-time jobs, have families, and are deeply involved in extensive vocational or family activities bearing little relationship to conventional college life. While most adult students in college have little interest in extra-curricular activities, they are often intensely interested in vocational counseling and have a strong desire for this type of assistance because of their adult responsibilities.

Few two-year college counselors spend all of their time counseling. Many of them have other responsibilities such as organizing, administering, and interpreting testing programs, supervising student clubs and organizations, conducting orientation programs for new students, coordinating financial aid programs, and maintaining placement services. The following description of a representative day has been submitted by Miss Barbara Hall, a counselor and coordinator of student activities at Kishwaukee College in Malta, Illinois. Most of her day is spent in the latter activity.

A Typical Junior College Counselor's Day

8:30–9:00	Arrive on campus. Check mailbox, let secretary know I am here for the day.

	Check appointment book for day's appointments. Check out records of students with whom I have appointments for today. Go to office (in another building—the Student Center).
9:00–9:30	Open mail. Bring desk calendar up to date with coming appointments and meetings. Distribute post college and university brochures, notices of coming events, O.K. posters for Center; remove outdated notices from Center bulletin boards. Check with Student Senate office for what's happening, crises, upcoming events to prepare for.
9:30–10:15	Appointment with student in regard to interpretation of his interest inventory.
10:15–10:25	Coffee with an English instructor.
10:25–11:10	Meeting with art instructors in regard to evaluation of Student Personnel Services for past year. (We are evaluating our division's work for the past year, and we have been asking for "well dones" and "areas for improvement" from every division on campus, as well as from individuals, both students and faculty.)
11:10–11:15	Reply to a telephone call concerning location of a room for a meeting of the English staff. (I am the clearing-house for meeting rooms and times.)
11:15–12:10	Organize on paper the graduation ceremonies program. (I am completely responsible for every phase of graduation.) (1) Check with Music department on music to be played. (2) Contact faculty senate president for faculty representative who will give invocation at graduation.
12:10–1:00	Lunch
1:00–3:00	Student Personnel Services staff meeting in regard to planning of changes to be made in Sociology 120 (the freshmen orientation course which the counselors teach—this coming year I will lead small groups).
3:00–3:10	Appointment with a student concerning registration for summer school.

3:10–3:30	Telephone call—instructor asking about a student's absence.
3:30–3:45	Appointment with a student in regard to participation in graduation.
3:45–4:00	Telephone call—printer calling about graduation program copy.
4:00–4:20	Meeting with the Business Manager about collection of outstanding graduation fees (Twenty-three graduates have not paid.)
4:20–4:30	Telephone call in regard to meeting room needed for the Vet's Club.
4:30–4:45	Let switchboard know that I am leaving for the day. Check in at Student Services for appointments for tomorrow morning. Since there are none, I cross out 9–11 A.M. so that I can sit in on two classes in Art to find out what students are learning in Art History, so I can better advise students about this curriculum. Go home.

RELATED STUDENT PERSONNEL WORK

Counseling is but one of the many services provided for two-year college students. Persons involved in the wider range of student services are often called "student personnel workers." A number of counselors, after experience in a two-year college counseling center, become administrators (directors or assistants) of these related services. Only a brief outline of the career opportunities in these areas will be given here, as a more complete description will be provided in the section on colleges and universities.

1. *Admissions work.* Most colleges appoint an admissions officer, whose responsibilities include making sure that prospective students meet certain minimal qualifications. In addition, admissions work in two-year colleges involves providing students with accurate information about the strengths and weaknesses of the institution—its programs, faculty, and the like. Admissions officers often travel to the high schools of prospective students to confer with their teachers and counselors and to perform recruiting functions. Prospective students and their parents often visit the campus at some time during the admissions procedure with questions for admission officers. While many two-year colleges maintain an "open-door" admissions policy (any high school

graduate or anyone who is 18 years of age can enter), admissions officers seek information about students that will enable them to determine who can best benefit from the preparation programs offered by their institution. Otherwise, the "open door" that encourages students to enroll becomes a revolving door for students who enter and fail at the end of the first or second term.

2. *Registrar work*. In two-year colleges the registrar has the responsibility for maintaining student records. Records of students' courses, grades, health, aptitudes, and personal background are kept. These records are used within the college and form a base of information which is released by the institution. Often this information has profound but little understood implications for a student's future education and vocation, including admission to further schooling and employment opportunities.

3. *Student activities service*. Two-year colleges usually provide a variety of student activities and organizations, including student government. An ever-present problem is to maintain some continuity in student organizations, as the student body changes at least every two years. Since few two-year college students live on campus, student organizations are often viewed as vehicles for engendering and facilitating school spirit, student interaction, and cohesiveness.

4. *Health services*. In some two-year colleges, counselors have become administrators of health services. However, most junior and community colleges provide little in the way of health services, on the grounds that their students reside at home and use family-connected services.

5. *Housing*. Residential two-year colleges often delegate to a director of housing the responsibility of running dormitories and the services provided.

6. *Discipline*. While many interpretations are available as to the meaning of discipline, most colleges have, within their student personnel program, an individual who is responsible for administering discipline to students who violate college regulations. Currently much effort is devoted to making sure that "due process" (ensuring student rights) is followed in disciplinary procedures.

PREPARATION REQUIRED

The preparation program for two-year college counseling usually includes coursework in the nature, services, philosophy, and development of junior colleges, as well as a counseling internship in such an institution. Otherwise, coursework and experience requirements are similar to those for other counselors.

Many two-year colleges employ counselors who have had secondary school counseling experience, while others employ entry-level counselors who have had a counseling internship in a junior or community college.

Currently most two-year college counselors have had at least one graduate year of counselor preparation. While some junior and community colleges require that their counselors be eligible to teach some courses (usually beginning psychology, sociology or study skills), few states, if any, have created certification requirements for such counselors.

WORKING CONDITIONS

Because many two-year colleges have been built in recent years, physical facilities for counseling are often excellent. However, in some junior and community colleges, the physical facilities have been unable to keep up with the rapidly expanding student enrollments and an attendant increase in staff members.

Many two-year college counseling centers maintain late afternoon and evening hours, since those are the times that most students are on campus and free to confer with counselors.

SALARIES

Few sources are available for estimating counselors' salaries in two-year colleges. It is estimated that counselors with a master's degree but little or no experience earn approximately $8,500 annually, while those with experience and further education range upward of $12,000 to $16,000. Because of increased responsibilities, counselors who become administrators of student personnel services often earn more.

CURRENT ISSUES

A continuing issue for two-year college counselors is the wisdom of the open-door admissions policy. Such a policy is, of course, one of the distinguishing characteristics of comprehensive community colleges. At the heart of the issue is whether such a policy means that no applicant can be denied admission to particular programs offered by the institution.

Some public colleges with access to a limited number of students have maintained an open-door admissions policy despite the fact that they lack educational programs appropriate to the wide range of abilities and interests of the students who are admitted. Other institutions, eager to stimulate larger enrollments, accept all who apply regardless of programs available. Furthermore, parents often argue that since they pay local taxes that support the two-year college, their sons and daughters have every right to attempt college-level work. For them college represents the means for their children to acquire the benefits of an affluent society. When counselors or admissions officers attempt to help students with below-average high school academic records and low college admissions test scores by relating these factors to the requirements in a transfer curriculum, they often meet disbelief and resistance. Such students (and their parents) often insist they will do better if given a chance to enter a community college, which represents an opportunity for them to turn over a new leaf.

Despite the financial pressures and community attitudes toward an open-door admissions policy, some community colleges selectively admit students to specific curricula, such as the transfer curriculum leading to further education in a four-year college. Often the two-year nursing curriculum requires students to demonstrate certain minimum performances on standardized tests as well as acceptable high school grades. Undoubtedly this issue will continue to be discussed and examined for some time. It seems safe to conclude that a community college could benefit more from a clear communication of and insistence on the requisite skills needed for a particular program than by failing large numbers of students at the end of the first term.

A second issue often argued by two-year college counselors is whether they should be given an academic rank (instructor, assistant or associate professor). Some two-year colleges do not give academic rank to any instructors, let alone counselors. However, counselors argue that where the teaching faculty is given academic rank—but not counselors—they suffer in their professional interchanges with faculty. Other counselors claim that if they are later employed by a university, their lack of rank places them at a disadvantage.

Arguments against giving counselors academic rank claim it should be reserved for the teaching faculty. Perhaps the issue could best be solved by making all appointments (custodians, counselors, teachers, administrators) at the rank of professor!

CAREER PATTERNS

Two-year college counselors often bring to the position previous counseling experience in secondary schools and other settings. The fluid status and ever-increasing numbers of junior colleges have drawn many counselors with a year or two of counseling experience, especially those with doctorates, into the administration of student personnel programs. It is not unusual for some later to become presidents of two-year colleges.

OUTLOOK

The future of two-year college counseling appears bright. More and more states are funding and building a system of community colleges that will be within commuting distance of every high school student. The claim is often made that one of the most important services such institutions can make available to students is counseling.

SOURCES OF FURTHER INFORMATION

Blocker, Clyde E.; Plummer, Robert H.; and Richardson, Richard C., Jr. *The Two-Year College: A Social Synthesis*. Englewood Cliffs, N.J.: Prentice-Hall, 1965. 298 pp.

The Carnegie Commission on Higher Education. *The Open-Door Colleges*. New York: McGraw-Hill Book Company, June 1970. 74 pp.

Gleazer, E. J. *This Is the Community College*. Boston: Houghton Mifflin Company, 1968.

Colleges and Universities

In its more than 350 years of existence, higher education in the United States has experienced remarkable expansion in size and variety. Higher education includes small and large private liberal arts colleges, large state universities, denominational colleges, municipal colleges and universities, and two-year colleges. Currently approximately 40 percent of the age bracket 18 to 24 years enter college, and the proportion of youth who do so continues upward each year. Great variety exists in American higher education—in standards and objectives, the curricula offered, how the institutions are organized, financed and controlled, and size and composition of the student body.

Today's American high school graduate has the option of applying to approximately 2,000 accredited colleges and universities. This magnitude and variety are a source of benefits and concern. The concern lies in the fact that people have come to value the process of college study more than the product, and in the fact that disagreement exists regarding the mission and financial arrangements established for universities. The gains or benefits include a flexibility that insures educational freedom and a willingness to experiment in curriculum and methods of instruction.

Counseling, broadly interpreted, has been conducted by many professorial and staff members on every campus since the beginnings of higher education. However, counselors as such came on the college scene after World War II to complement the faculty advising of students. Prior to their entry, personnel officers were appointed. For example, in about 1890 the first student dean of men at Harvard and the first dean of women at the University of Chicago and Oberlin were the forerunners of student personnel workers and college counselors. The evolution of organized counseling services in higher education institutions has not been smoothly progressive, direct, or simple.

The impetus for employing trained counselors who devoted their full time to this task came after World War II, when many veterans entered college. Veterans counseling centers were established on most college campuses. Today it is unusual to find a college or university without either a highly centralized counseling center with a cadre of full-time, professional counselors or decentralized counseling services provided within its departments or schools, housing operations, dean of student offices, or student health services. Many universities maintain a centralized counseling center offering psychological services as well as faculty curriculum advising within departments or schools. Student counselors often are employed within housing units, and psychiatric services are offered within the student health center.

NATURE OF THE COLLEGE COUNSELOR'S WORK

The typical college counselor counsels students in need of educational, vocational, and personal help and often is involved in "how-to-study" programs, orientation activities, state-wide high school testing programs, providing internship experiences for graduate counseling students, consulting with dormitory counselors, and a host of other activities. The pattern of their work shows much variation from one campus to another, and a "typical" college counselor would be hard to find.

However, the functions most often conducted by college counselors are educational counseling on choice of major or curriculum, vocational counseling based on understanding one's aptitudes and other personality and environmental factors, and personal counseling focusing on social "adjustment" and understanding of self and others. Both individual and group counseling approaches are utilized.

Surveys of college counseling centers have revealed that their counselors (1) serve approximately 2,000 students each, (2) have counseling contacts with about 10 to 12 percent of the student body each year, (3) administer tests (counseling is not involved) to students for the administrative or academic departments, (4) provide some group counseling experiences for students, (5) engage in training residence hall staff, (6) become involved in orientation programs, (7) supervise doctoral students in counseling, and (8) provide assistance to students with reading and study difficulties.

Currently many college counselors are actively seeking ways that will enable them to have a greater impact on the student body. In some colleges this has taken the form of providing human relations training or some type of group experiences in housing units; in others, such "outreach" activities have been through establishing crisis telephone services or teaching mini-courses on human relations, drug abuse, marriage, and the like.

David Novicki, a counselor at the University of Evansville (Indiana) has supplied an account of a day's activities.

A Typical Day as a College Counselor

8:00–9:00	The period 8:00–9:00 is maintained as a time free of appointments to be used for reviewing schedule and case notes for the coming day. This takes about 20 to 30 minutes, and the remaining time is spent answering correspondence over a second cup of coffee.
9:00–9:45	Counseling session with a 24-year-old male senior at the college. This is his seventh session, and I have been seeing him on a weekly basis. His central problem appears to be a lack of self-confidence and motivation, a fear of graduation (this is his second year with senior hours and he still does not have enough hours in any particular area to complete a major), and poor relationships with significant others, particularly his wife.
9:45–10:00	End of counseling session. I dictate case notes before my 10:00 appointment.
10:00–10:55	Counseling session with a 29-year-old male sophomore who returned to college this past fall, ten years after dropping out following his freshman year. He has been doing mediocre academic work and has recently completed a vocational evaluation through this office. As a result of the content of the evaluation sessions, it has appeared that further psychological counseling would be advantageous. Today's session is the first of a number of contacts.
10:55–11:00	End of a slightly longer than average session and the hasty dictation of case notes.
11:00–12:50	Meet with the Director of Residence Hall Counseling for the purpose of exploring further directions her staff could take to assist in the development of a positive mental health atmosphere for the campus. This meeting breaks at approximately 11:45 A.M. and leaves me with the opportunity to get home for a quick lunch rather than eating on campus.
12:50–1:15	Return to the office to review the morning mail and return telephone calls.
1:15–2:15	Counseling session with a 17-year-old male freshman. This individual is involved in regular counseling sessions as a result of a referral from a

member of the residence hall counseling staff because of poor relationships and conflicts with others, particularly his roommate. This is the third session in what is projected to be a lengthy, intense counseling relationship.

2:15–2:50 A referral from the University Academic Advising Committee has come for vocational-educational counseling. He is an 18-year-old male freshman engineering student who has come for the appointment because he was sent here; he is not interested in counseling. He believes that while his grades are mediocre, he can do better by taking a lighter class load and seeking extra help.

2:50–3:20 Coffee break at Student Union with co-facilitator of T-group; although we have already discussed the previous group and have related ideas about this evening's group, we briefly recheck signals. It is a nice day, so we end up outside chatting.

3:20–3:30 I return to the office and check telephone calls. One call is returned to the Dean of Women regarding a person she had referred earlier. The Dean of Women was interested in knowing whether or not the girl had continued the counseling relationship. I responded affirmatively.

3:30–4:30 Counseling session with an 18-year-old female freshman. Core problem related to feelings of loneliness and lack of friends, particularly male friends. Discomfort with her perception of herself in the traditional role of a woman. Dictate case notes.

4:30–4:45 Dictate memo to Director of the Center regarding summer vacation. Case folders and dictation tape given to secretary for filing and processing.

4:45–6:20 Leave office for a quick dinner.

6:20–6:30 Return to office for evening T-group. T-group has been operational for eight weeks. Co-facilitator is already at the office and busy making coffee for the evening.

6:30–9:45 Meet with the group. In general this evening's group session is somewhat more intense than expected. One of the group members has made the decision to quit the group this evening and is very set in his decision. The time involved in his leaving the group is about an hour with a great deal of emotion expressed. After the departure, the group is silent for about 45 minutes then enters a period of discussion of feelings about the departure of the member. Most of the thought and feelings about the person who left and the departure itself are resolved about 9:45 P.M., and the group decides to stop for the evening.

9:45–10:00 The co-facilitators also decide to call it a night after deciding on a time to get together the following day to review the process of the group.

RELATED CAREER OPPORTUNITIES

The work of a university counselor is viewed as but one of many student personnel services that exist on every college campus. These allied occupations represent career opportunities that should be examined by anyone who is interested in providing a helping relationship for college students. Some of these services are identical to those earlier described for two-year colleges. The additions here seek to amplify the description of career opportunities within higher education:

1. *Foreign student advising.* The migration of students to international centers of learning has been common for centuries, but it is only since World War II that American colleges and universities have played a prominent part in the education of persons who leave their home to study abroad. Probably one hundred or so colleges educate 70 percent of the approximately 40,000 foreign students in this country. Foreign student offices have been established on most university campuses to provide (1) pre-arrival negotiations and travel plans and documents, (2) housing arrangements, and (3) educational evaluation and placement, including language proficiency evaluation. Counselors who serve foreign students walk a tightrope between oversolicitude and caring concern. Foreign students are a very heterogeneous group but share one thing in common: being away from home. Because of their diversity, what causes difficulty for one may offer no problem for another. However, every personnel worker knows that holiday periods pose problems for foreign students if they are lonely, homesick, or idle. Advisors also know that they must guard against the exploitation of foreign students by the social and professional clubs of the local community. Persons who work with these students must have

great understanding, tremendous sources of energy, flexibility, and objectivity.

2. *Financial aid and student employment.* Most colleges have established an office to administer and consolidate the many sources of financial aid available to students. Today's financial aid officers endeavor to develop a "package" consisting of scholarship, loan, and part-time work funds based on demonstrated financial need for each student. The types of student aid—fellowships, scholarships, grants, loans, student employment, teaching, and research assistantships—grow yearly in volume, and the administration and best distribution of such aid become ever more complex.

All too often, financial aid officers seem more concerned about business investments and efficiency rather than the type of aid which will contribute most to a particular student's development. Professionals who work with students seek to translate into practice the ideal that the student should receive the kind of financial aid best suited to nurture his personal and intellectual development and that the student's financial need, abilities, and future development must be considered in deciding the amount of aid he receives.

Career opportunities for persons who seek to work in this field are abundant. Positions are available as financial counselors and as administrators or directors of the program. Persons who enter the field work closely with others involved in student personnel services across the campus as well as directly with students.

3. *Placement service.* Programs directed toward the placement of college graduates into permanent positions of employment are recognized student personnel responsibilities. While any number of routes may be used by the college senior to obtain his first position after graduation, prominent among them is the campus placement office. University placement services provide interviewing schedules; filing, duplicating, and dispensing placement credentials; establishing and cultivating job opportunities with the "outside" world; and a host of other activities. Placement bureaus, concerned because they have long functioned merely as referral offices, are currently striving to provide better vocational counseling services to their student and alumni clientele. Persons employed in placement offices spend much time in interpreting

their services to students and to employers. It is a service that seeks to bring together students and their interests, professors and their recommendations, employers and their job openings.

4. *Student discipline.* The responsibility for student discipline is often located in the office of the Dean of Students, Dean of Men, or Dean of Women. Persons charged with this function work with individuals and groups to conduct and prevent campus misbehavior. Treatment for campus misbehavior is often divided into several categories such as financial irregularities (nonpayment of debts, bad checks), minor misconduct (dispute with householders), disorderly conduct (drunkenness, gambling, destroying property, reckless driving), sexual misconduct (pregnancies, promiscuity), theft and burglary, misuse of privileges, cheating, drug abuse.

The work of disciplinarians usually includes investigating the facts and decisions pertaining to a course of action. Most universities have established administrative policies and practices for handling disciplinary cases. If disciplinary situations are viewed as learning situations, then the student is often referred first to a counselor to help him gain insight into his behavior and possible rehabilitation. If the counselor fails, or if the offense requires protective action by the academic community, the counselor or the student requests referral of the case to judicial committees. College disciplinarians today are searching for practices and procedures which will guarantee and protect the rights of a student but which will avoid entanglement in complex legal procedures designed for civil and criminal proceedings.

5. *Student activities.* Student activities are usually viewed as a means to (1) continue and enhance the individual's socialization process, (2) provide opportunities for experiencing group interaction, and (3) develop leaders. In reality, a large part of the education of the college student goes on outside the classroom in his social life. This informal social "curriculum" contributes to his personal development. The scope and range of the college activities program are vast, requiring many individuals to administer the program. Such personnel are responsible for scheduling campus activities, approving and coordinating social events, and consulting with student leaders. Persons in charge of the activities

program need to possess management skills, friendly tolerance, and the ability to get along with people.

6. *Orientation service. Orientation,* as applied to student personnel services, means assisting students in acquiring the techniques of living in college, in achieving a beneficial balance among all the demands and opportunities of college life, and in gaining a perspective and sense of purpose. The primary objective of orientation activities is to acquaint students with the physical facilities and the available instructional and recreational services, as well as the college's traditions and standards. Usually, orientation activities are conducted prior to the student's move to the campus during "freshmen days" or during the first term. Some colleges have orientation courses that include adjustment to college, development of reading, studying and test-taking skills, educational and vocational planning.

7. *Student housing.* Individuals employed in this area seek to (1) provide physical accommodations, (2) promote academic learning, and (3) enhance the personal development of students. Their work includes administration of residence halls, supervising personnel staff, coordinating residence hall counselors, and providing services to those who live off-campus.

8. *Admissions.* The recruitment, selection, and admission of students have become highly specialized tasks, for this function sometimes determines the "life or death" of the institution. Professionals employed in admissions offices work with faculty and administrators to determine policies for admitting students, establish cooperative relationships with secondary school personnel, process application materials, and confer with interested students and their parents. Admissions officers make many visits to high schools and, in turn, schedule visits of high school students and counselors to the campus.

9. *Registrar.* The administration of student records (maintenance, storage, retrieval) is a function which serves both the institution and the student. Personnel records are used in the general administration of the college to provide statistics needed for financing and planning and in counseling, planning, and placement relationships with students.

Summary. The positions described here are usually part of what is normally called student personnel work. The structure of these offices varies greatly from college to college. In many colleges, personnel who administer each of these services report to a vice president of student services or a dean of students. In other colleges, some offices report directly to the president. Essentially, personnel work seeks to relate individual students to the vast and complicated resources of the institution so that they may contribute constructively to the student's educational experience.

PREPARATION REQUIRED

While the Ph.D. degree is commonly held by counselors employed in a centralized university counseling center, it usually is not required for counseling positions associated with individual departments, schools, and other such offices. Many professional counselors with a master's degree and previous experience in counseling are employed in colleges and universities.

There are no state certification requirements for counselors employed in colleges. The college, of course, can and does prescribe the criteria—preparation, experience, etc.—for the position.

The content of programs of professional education which prepare student personnel workers has been outlined by a committee representing several professional organizations[2] whose model for developing a preparation program contains the following parts:

1. Student personnel work in higher education—an overview of the profession, including its history, philosophy, purposes, issues, and ethics.
2. Higher education as a social institution—knowledge of the college setting, its organization and administration, objectives, environmental presses, and curricula.
3. Human growth and development—the nature and needs of the college student's development.

[2] American College Personnel Association, Association of Counselor Education and Supervision, Council of Student Personnel Associations in Higher Education, Association of Student Personnel Administrators in Teacher Education, American Association of Collegiate Registrars and Admissions Officers, Association of College Unions, Association of College and University Housing Offices, National Association of Women Deans and Counselors, National Association of Student Personnel Administrators, the College Placement Council.

4. Social and cultural foundations—studies of change, use of leisure time, cultural mores, and various life patterns of men and women.
5. Methods, techniques, and concepts—counseling principles, theories and techniques, group processes, decision-making, organizational and fiscal management.
6. Research and evaluation—to understand and apply statistics, research methods, and tests and measurements to student personnel work.
7. Preparation in specialized fields—knowledge of admissions, financial aid, housing, etc.; students' roles and rights; legal and social issues.[3]

WORKING CONDITIONS

The position or status of the counselor or student personnel worker in the campus community depends primarily on his training and his place in the personnel staff, as well as his assignments and the way he succeeds in accomplishing them. His schedule is usually full, requiring him to work long hours. Interviews, committees, and correspondence leave him little leisure time. He is usually employed on a 12-month rather than a 10-month schedule.

University counselors and personnel workers are usually viewed as performing a "service" function as opposed to teaching or research, which are more highly prized and rewarded on most campuses. As such, their salary raises and advancement and tenure considerations vary widely from campus to campus.

SALARIES

Beginning salaries for most college counselors and student personnel workers with a master's degree average $8,500 for 12-month contracts. Counselors with doctoral degrees and prior counseling and work experience usually start at approximately $11,000 annually.

CURRENT ISSUES

A major issue confronting college counselors is whether their work should be confined to students who come to their office

[3] "Guidelines for Graduate Programs in the Preparation of Student Personnel Workers in Higher Education." *Personnel and Guidance Journal,* Vol. 47 (January 1969), pp. 493–498.

with remedial or crisis situations, or expanded and conducted in such a way that a greater impact on the student body is achieved in the area of personal development. Some have characterized this issue as a question of whether a counseling center should be composed of individuals whose major functions tend to be *reactive* (assisting students to make educational and vocational choices, crisis counseling, and brief psychotherapy) or *proactive* (reaching out through intensive group counseling, marathon groups, and consultation with housing units). Most progressive university counseling centers seem to be attempting to do both.

Another issue and source of conflict between college administrators and directors of college counseling centers regards the confidentiality of student records. Some college administrators believe that counselors should provide information to them, for example, about student clients who are or who might become involved in disciplinary infractions or academic probation. Other administrators feel counseling information should be shared with faculty or prospective employers. Such practices in which information about clients is made available to outside persons or agencies without the client's knowledge or permission are not congruent with the ethical code of the APGA.

CAREER PATTERNS

Generally, college counselors and student personnel workers with master's degrees have little vertical mobility without additional preparation. Counselors with doctoral degrees often move into administrative, supervisory, and teaching positions as director of counseling centers, dean of students, director of admissions, registrar, or director of housing. They may also engage in part-time teaching or research and then eventually pursue this activity on a full-time basis.

OUTLOOK

Entry-level student personnel positions (student activities, housing, admissions, financial aids) promise to remain in strong demand. Some contraction will undoubtedly occur in entry-level counseling positions, as well as those requiring the doctorate, with the increased supply of counselors prepared in the area. Adverse economic conditions influencing college enrollments and college funding undoubtedly will play their part in the supply and demand for counselors and student personnel workers at this level.

Summary

Counselors in all educational settings perform similar functions: counseling, consulting, assessment, and coordinating functions. They represent a group of professionals committed to establishing and maintaining helping relationships with those the institution is designed to serve—individual students in pursuit of intellectual and personal development.

Surely, the position of the counselor can be viewed now as firmly established in most educational settings (secondary schools and colleges) and rapidly developing in others (elementary schools and vocational schools). There is little doubt that students at every level of education have certain ever-present needs—for clarification of self and educational and vocational endeavors—that can be responded to through the helping relationships extended by counselors. Presently, in many schools and colleges, counseling practitioners are no longer asked to justify their existence and can devote their full time to providing services. Today's demand for accountability for expenditures through demonstrated outcomes in the educational enterprise also affects counseling services. Counselors everywhere seek to make sure their services are responsive to the needs and requirements of the student population they serve as well as the goals of the institution in which they are employed. Much remains to be done to refine techniques and procedures as well as to improve counseling services in educational settings. It is especially important to determine which counselors and techniques work best with certain clients in given situations.

CAREER COUNSELING OPPORTUNITIES IN THE FEDERAL, STATE, AND LOCAL GOVERNMENT

CHAPTER 4

Schools and colleges are not the only settings in which counselors are employed. The material in this chapter and the next presents the work of counselors in settings other than education.

Vocational Rehabilitation

The Vocational Rehabilitation Administration, a federal agency within the Department of Health, Education, and Welfare, provides leadership and coordination as well as sponsoring research and demonstration projects in vocational rehabilitation. In addition, it distributes and administers matching funds for divisional offices located in the various states and territories.

Rehabilitation programs—initiated in 1918 for veterans and extended in 1920 to civilians—were characterized by modest growth until World War II, when the nation began to recognize its obligation to disabled veterans. The public program for vocational rehabilitation is a partnership of the federal and state governments: services are provided to disabled persons by the state vocational rehabilitation agencies with financial assistance from the federal government. Vocational rehabilitation is a public service in the same sense as the school systems, libraries, police, and fire departments.

A public rehabilitation program is available in every state. Each state maintains regional offices located geographically to serve various segments of the population.

The Vocational Rehabilitation Administration estimates that millions of men, women, and children in the United States are afflicted with physical and mental disabilities which are neglected. For example, some 18 million children are estimated to have significant disabilities or crippling conditions, including 10.2 million in need of eye care. Currently about 200,000 men and women are receiving rehabilitation services aimed to help them overcome dependency and idleness and to enjoy a rewarding life. *Rehabilitation* has been defined as the restoration of the handicapped to their full capacity of physical, mental, and vocational usefulness. Disabled individuals want and need to work; vocational rehabilitation services exist to translate this need and will into the ability to be gainfully employed. Essentially, the vocational rehabilitation service involves identifying individuals with handicaps; providing for correction or modification of the handicap through physical therapy, surgery, prosthetic limbs, or training; and providing placement in an appropriate occupation.

Uniform criteria of eligibility for rehabilitation services have been established by each state as prescribed by the regulations of the Federal Vocational Rehabilitation Department. Individuals with disabilities resulting from birth, accident, disease, or emotional causes are eligible for services. These handicaps may include arm and leg deformities, amputations, heart and lung ailments, defects of hearing, speech and vision, mental illness and retardation as well as other handicapping conditions. The disability does not have to be visible, but regulations stipulate that its presence must limit the individual in his activities. In general, to be eligible for services from a state office of vocational rehabilitation, one must (1) have a disability that substantially interferes with employment, (2) have a reasonable chance of becoming suitably employed within a reasonable time period, and (3) be within an employable age range when rehabilitation services are completed.

Vocational rehabilitation services include the following:

1. *Medical examination.* A medical examination is required by regulations to determine eligibility for services.

The examination is conducted for all who apply in order to determine the extent of disability, to discover hidden disabilities, and to ascertain work capacity.

2. *Assessment and counseling.* Client assessment includes evaluation of his education, mental ability, interests, recreational pursuits, work history, achievements, personality patterns, social adjustment, family relationships, and the like. If appropriate, clients receive personal and vocational counseling.

3. *Surgical, psychiatric, and/or hospital treatment.* These services are provided, if needed, to the disabled. Public funds are used if the individual is unable to pay part or all of the costs.

4. *Education and/or training.* This includes education or training in schools, colleges, on-the-job, tutoring, or correspondence courses. Maintenance and transportation costs, fees, books, tuition, and supplies may be provided, depending on the state plan.

5. *Artificial limbs, hearing aids, and braces.* Various prosthetic devices are supplied if needed.

6. *Transportation, tools, licenses, and occupational equipment.* These are available if necessary for employment in a particular occupation.

7. *Placement and follow-up.* Individuals are placed in employment settings with follow-up counseling to make sure they are in appropriate positions and that they are adjusting to the demands of the job.

NATURE OF THE REHABILITATION COUNSELOR'S WORK

The rehabilitation counselor is employed in a variety of settings: agencies, hospitals, labor unions, special schools, sheltered workshops, Veterans Administration centers. Each setting exerts some influence on what the counselor does. In the past, counseling as such occupied a relatively small proportion of the counselor's time; rather, he coordinated cases and purchased services from other specialists. Today the emphasis has shifted to more counseling and evaluation by the rehabilitation counselor.

The vocational rehabilitation counselor is responsible for locating clientele, determining their eligibility, collecting, collating, and analyzing data, working with clients to develop vocational goals, and helping them to establish a rehabilitation plan. In the initial interview, the vocational counselor establishes a working relationship with the individual, conveys information about the vocational rehabilitation program, and, if the individual is eligible for services, provides assistance in completing an application for services.

Usually a plan of rehabilitation is worked out jointly by the counselor, the client, and persons who provide medical treatment, occupational training, and other required special services. Additional interviews are conducted with the client to discuss his program, to check on his progress, and to help resolve problems he encounters. Emphasis is placed on the dynamic forces influencing vocational choice and adjustment as well as the psychological factors involved in implementing training or vocational goals. Often psychological testing is conducted to determine interests and aptitudes as well as to help the disabled person establish occupational objectives. Fundamentally, counseling is viewed as a means of modifying the client's attitudes and behavior so that he can progress toward vocational planning, choice, or adjustment in training and employment.

The time spent in direct counseling varies with the individual and his attitudes toward his disability, as well as with the counselor's case-load. Experienced rehabilitation counselors usually are responsible for many persons at various stages of rehabilitation, while inexperienced counselors may handle relatively few cases at a time. When the client is ready for employment, the counselor assists him in finding a suitable job and makes follow-up visits to ascertain the appropriateness of the placement and the individual's adjustment to the work.

While assessment and counseling are the major functions of rehabilitation counseling, other functions are performed which support and complement counseling. Chief among these is the counselor's efforts to reach out to prospective clients and the community, and to influence placement possibilities. He must maintain close contact with other professional people working with handicapped persons, members of the client's family, other agencies (particularly schools), and civic groups. Most counselors, by necessity, conduct a vigorous program to educate employers about hiring handicapped individuals and carry on publicity throughout the community about the rehabilitation program.

Mrs. Celeste Dye, a former vocational rehabilitation counselor in California, reported the following activities as representing a typical day for her:

A Typical Day as a Vocational Rehabilitation Counselor

8:00–9:00 I check my mailbox, dictate correspondence, and return telephone calls. After getting coffee, I enter appointments on the work calendar and dictate intake appraisals, progress notes, and summaries for the clients' charts.

9:00–10:00 Client "C" with his mother. The first client of the day is an 18-year-old Caucasian male, earlier referred by the hospital out-patient clinic. He had been diagnosed as mentally retarded in childhood and has attended numerous schools for the handicapped. Previous sessions with this client have suggested that efforts directed toward fostering his independence have met with disapproval from his mother. Consequently it seemed advisable to ask his mother to come in with her son. The session provided the mother with an opportunity to explore her need to protect her son from failure and situations involving possible failure. She and her son discuss some of their feelings about this sheltering, and we decide that our workshop might be appropriate in determining the client's ability for independent functioning. In addition, it will enable us to determine if the limited vision in his right eye is a serious impediment to his eye-hand coordination. Previous intelligence testing has raised questions about the extent of his "retardation," since his scores range between 90 and 100. In counseling sessions he appears more socially than mentally retarded, and in discussing the test results he expresses his feelings about being diagnosed as retarded and the implications of this social stigma. He seems highly motivated and is anxious to begin in the workshop as soon as possible. While he is being evaluated there, I will be investigating placement in job training opportunities for him.

10:00–10:15 I arrange with shop supervisor for the referral of client "C" beginning the following Monday. Dictate progress note for file.

10:15–11:00 Client "A" is a 48-year-old male amputee referred from the surgical ward for vocational counseling and placement. His vocational history does not demonstrate any prior serious career choice but merely selection by circumstance. His personal history reveals a long-standing problem of alcoholism, which has affected relations with his family and his employers. Vocational and intelligence testing has indicated sufficient ability for electronics assembly, and counseling with the client has suggested it as a feasible choice. Client has been in work evaluation for the past two weeks and, despite his lack of speed, demonstrates sufficient aptitude and motivation to be considered a placement candidate. He is well liked by fellow workers but reveals feelings of inadequacy which also show up in our counseling sessions. Past sessions have moved slowly toward today's discussion of his self-concept and his past inability to achieve what he wants. We focus on his successes, which seems to cheer him up despite the intermittent periods of remorse following each disclosure. His feelings of inadequacy had, in the past, kept him from revealing significant aspects of himself, but today some trust has developed. When he leaves he seems genuinely pleased and asks me to stop by this afternoon to see his work.

11:00–12:15 I write a quick progress note on "A" and head for the hospital ward for the inpatient vocational counseling group. Many of the group members have been slow in revealing their feelings about themselves as workers and in learning to trust each other and the group. We spend the hour dealing with the anger and frustration of two members who feel that "life" has crippled them and left them unable to deal with "society." Other members offer warmth and encouragement, but the group as a whole, I feel, has a long way to go.

12:15–1:00 Lunch with a friend working with Chicano dropouts. Conversation shifts quickly from Chicanos and handicapped clients to less weighty issues.

1:00–1:40 I stop on the ward to enter progress notes on patients' charts. Dr. J., the unit surgeon, is there, and we discuss a recent amputee's problem of stump deterioration and what it might mean to his recovery. We agree that counseling sessions should be directed toward shifting the focus from the stump back to the whole individual. The counselor-aide trainee accompanies me this afternoon to "learn the ropes." We stop at Physical Therapy to find out if another client is exhibiting motivation in that setting, and learn from the therapist that motivation is only marginal. I note this for a future session with the client. We move on to a clerical "work station" where the client and her supervisor are equally pleased with her performance and initiative. The client beams with pride and I am very happy for her.

1:40–2:15 We check in at the workshop and Work Evaluation Center. Client "J," referred from the state psychiatric hospital, receives a good rating from his supervisor. His specially-structured work situation has shown us that he can function productively and independently without aggressive behavior, and the client is extremely pleased with himself. For this individual, psychoneurosis has not ruled out the possibility of gainful employment in a structured work environment.

We stop by to see "A" and the electronic equipment he has been tearing down, and he demonstrates how several parts work. The Work Evaluation supervisor comes in and we jointly decide to set up skills testing on specific aspects of the task. I note these for follow-up during a field visit to a possible training school for "A."

2:15–3:00 Brief initial session with client "M," a 50-year-old single woman who had been struck by a car. She had lost her right leg and was referred by the surgical unit supervisor for counseling. We spend the period discussing her apprehension about resuming a normal life and the impact this trauma has had on her already lonely existence. She seems easily frightened and changes topics rapidly. She suggests some topics which she needs to discuss and we plan our next session.

3:00–4:00 I map out two field visits, alert the counselor-aide, Bob, and we head out. An on-the-job visit to client "R," who was placed in a bench-assembly task at an aluminum small parts factory six weeks ago. Both he and his shop foreman are quite pleased with his work, and he has already received a raise of $4 per week. A quick "hello" to the personnel director and we continue on.

4:00–4:50 We visit a possible training school for client "A." Bob makes notes on transportation arrangements as we drive, and checks the physical plant for wheelchair access, after we arrive. "A" has partial ambulation on his prosthesis but must still depend largely on his wheelchair for mobility. We examine the facilities with the owner-manager and discuss the curriculum and program fees. He is vague about placement upon graduation, but our service has developed a fairly sophisticated placement program to use for these situations. We make notes on specific factors to check on in work evaluation in the morning. Drop Bob back at his car and head home.

PREPARATION REQUIRED

Generally, vocational rehabilitation counselors are college graduates with graduate course credit in counseling, psychology, sociology, and related fields. While standard requirements have yet to be established, much uniformity exists in graduate-level counseling programs for rehabilitation across the country. Two years are usually required to complete the master's degree in rehabilitation counseling, a program offered by approximately 60 universities through training grants provided by the Vocational Rehabilitation Administration. These federally supported preparation programs recently have been curtailed somewhat due to a reduction in the availability of federal funds. As an example of the coursework and experiences required, the University of Southern California's training program includes:

First Semester:

Introduction to Rehabilitation

Vocational Theory and Processes

Counseling Theory and Procedures

Measurement Theories and Procedures in Counseling

Medical Aspects of Rehabilitation

Field Work Assignment (several, short-term)

Second Semester:

Introduction to Group Counseling

Seminar in Vocational Counseling and Placement

Statistics

Socio-Psychological Aspects of Disability

Practicum in Counseling

Field Work Assignment (one agency, six hours per week)

Third Semester:

Internship in Rehabilitation Counseling (20 hours per week)

Dynamics of Behavior

Case Practices in Rehabilitation

Master's Thesis Seminar

Elective

Fourth Semester:

Internship in Rehabilitation Counseling (20 hours per week)

Seminar in Counseling as a Profession

Master's Seminar

Electives

Increasingly, employers are requiring the master's degree as the minimum educational standard for professional rehabilitation counselors. Prior experience in social work, psychology, nursing, or education is given considerable weight, especially if an applicant has only a bachelor's degree.

Doctoral programs in rehabilitation counseling require two to four years of graduate work beyond the master's degree. Intensive preparation at this level is given in psychology, the social and biological sciences, and research. A supervised internship of at least one year in a rehabilitation center is required.

WORKING CONDITIONS

The working conditions vary considerably for the 12,000 counselors employed in state agencies, hospitals, special schools, insurance companies, sheltered workshops, Veterans Administration centers, and other public and private agencies providing rehabilitation services. The physical facilities are generally good. Counselors usually work a 12-month year and a 40-hour week, or slightly less, with little paid overtime. However, educational and public relations activities within the community occupy many evenings.

The practicing vocational rehabilitation counselor often finds himself overburdened with a caseload of approximately 125 to 150 clients, plus an unending intake flow. Many counselors, especially in government agencies, complain about the mountain of paperwork, reports, and authorizations that accompany their work. Others strain against the constant pressure to produce the so-called "26 closures" (rehabilitation and placement within 26 weeks) established by federal and state regulations.

About 75 percent of the state rehabilitation agencies require that applicants meet state civil service and merit regulations. Such regulations require the individual to pass written competitive examinations. Additionally, a board of examiners often conducts evaluative interviews with applicants.

SALARIES

Beginning salaries for rehabilitation counselors range from $6,000 to $8,500 annually. Counselors with doctorates earn from $12,000 to $15,000, depending on experience and other variables.

CURRENT ISSUES

A persistent issue among rehabilitation counselors is whether their major function is as a counselor or as a coordinator of services for disabled individuals. Those who view counseling as their primary function argue that counselors specialize in helping disabled clients with serious problems of personal adjustment. They acknowledge that many of the clientele served by rehabilitation services do not need long-term counseling. They argue further that where rehabilitation service coordination is needed, it could be conducted by paraprofessionals, thereby freeing the counselor to concentrate on patients who require extensive counseling.

Rehabilitation counselors who view themselves as coordinators of services believe that case management is the counselor's major function. In short, counselors exist to facilitate each case as rapidly and effectively as possible. As a coordinator of services, the counselor's major function is to purchase services available in the community that are needed by the client, including psychotherapy.

This issue has been debated for some time and seems unlikely to be resolved, given the diverse prior experience and preparation of persons who serve as rehabilitation counselors.

Another current issue is whether job placement of rehabilitated clients is an appropriate function of vocational rehabilitation counselors. Some counselors argue that as professional counselors they should concentrate fully on counseling. They view placement in an occupation as a separate task to be performed by paraprofessionals or by an Employment Service office (see the following section on U.S. Training and Employment Service). Others argue that placement of a disabled person cannot be separated from the total rehabilitation process, and that for this reason it is an appropriate responsibility of the counselor.

Related to this issue is the question of whether the goal of vocational rehabilitation is vocational adjustment (interpreted as placement in an occupation) or some improved level of functioning by the client in society. The goal of vocational rehabilitation services has long been to enable the individual to work and to be self-supporting, for employment enables the individual to feel independent, competent, and useful. This issue may have emerged because rehabilitation centers have recently accepted clients with serious mental, emotional, or physical disabilities or socioeconomic disadvantages which make it difficult to achieve placement—traditionally considered the criterion of success for a particular case.

CAREER PATTERNS

Many individuals who enter the field of vocational rehabilitation as counselor-aides or paraprofessionals have the opportunity to acquire further preparation and become professional counselors. Vocational rehabilitation counselors often specialize in certain disabilities which may include mental retardation, alcoholism, drug addiction, speech and hearing impairments, or congenital deformities. Others move into research, supported by grant programs, on vocational rehabilitation problems to discover new principles, concepts, and approaches. Still others assume administrative positions in agencies after several years of experience as counselors.

OUTLOOK

The outlook for vocational rehabilitation counseling is extremely promising throughout the 1970's. The supply of qualified counselors in relation to the demand has long been inadequate. The Rehabilitation Services Administration estimates that at least 3,000 new counselors will be needed annually during this decade to meet new and expanded programs and to replace counselors who leave the profession. Because available vocational rehabilitation services have advanced faster than the programs preparing rehabilitation counselors, training grants have been established to support students and to increase the supply of counselors. While the funds for rehabilitation education training programs were reduced somewhat in early 1971, in the past they have helped to bring individuals into rehabilitation counseling who might otherwise not have entered.

The bright future demand for counselors in rehabilitation services can be traced to many factors including population growth as well as the extension of services to greater numbers of more severely disabled persons and to persons handicapped by social and economic disadvantages. Public educational efforts have begun to bear fruit so that handicapped individuals now have access to a greater variety of employment settings following rehabilitation services.

SOURCES OF FURTHER INFORMATION

Information on rehabilitation counseling can be secured from the following organizations:

American Psychological Association
1200 17th Street, N.W.
Washington, D.C. 20036

American Rehabilitation Counseling Association
1607 New Hampshire Avenue, N.W.
Washington, D.C. 20009

National Rehabilitation Counseling Association
1522 K Street, N.W.
Washington, D.C. 20005

U.S. Training and Employment Service

Public employment services designed to assist individuals in securing jobs have been in existence since 1907, when the federal government created the United States Employment Service (USES). The original purpose of the USES was to help immigrants find employment. In 1933, the Wagner-Peyser Act established a national system of employment offices for "men, women, and juniors." Large numbers of individuals, many of whom had little idea of their capabilities, were seeking assistance; to meet this need counselors were appointed in employment offices, particularly those in the larger cities. However, the critical labor shortages accompanying World War II brought a curtailment of counseling services. Emphasis was placed on the recruitment, utilization, and allocation of manpower for the war effort. Despite this curtailment in counseling, the years 1939 through 1946 were a productive period; for it was during this time that the Employment Service developed a number of counseling adjuncts such as job analysis, interviewing guides, the General Aptitude Test Battery, the *Dictionary of Occupational Titles,* and other counseling aids. Currently about 2,000 local offices across the nation locate employment opportunities, place job applicants, and select individuals for training and retraining programs. In 1968, approximately 11 million persons sought to make use of their services. It is estimated that about 4,400 full-time and 900 part-time counselors are currently employed in state Employment Service offices.

NATURE OF THE EMPLOYMENT COUNSELOR'S WORK

The nature of the counseling service provided by local offices of the U.S. Employment Service is shaped by its ultimate goal, to place individuals in jobs. Counselors engage in the following activities:

1. *Collection of labor market information.* Needs, changes, and trends in the employment situation at local, state, and national levels are assessed regularly. This information is collected and pooled at state and national levels and returned to the local offices to be made available to persons seeking jobs.

2. *Screening, evaluation, and classification.* If appropriate, applicants are provided with information about themselves through aptitude tests, interest inventories, trade and proficiency tests, and other inventories. Employment counselors use such data along with information collected through interviews to classify individuals occupationally so that appropriate referrals can be made and so that applicants can have an improved understanding of themselves and their vocational possibilities. Testing is used only if the counselor feels that it will facilitate this process. Data from the General Aptitude Test Battery permit a comparison of the individual's aptitudes in nine areas with aptitude requirements in various occupations.

3. *Counseling.* Applicants with no previous work experience or who have difficulty in securing and holding employment are offered counseling services. Counseling is provided also for individuals with a wide variety of problems including: choosing a vocation; acquiring suitable work patterns and attitudes; overcoming the effects of an impoverished background on personal adjustment; or establishing longer range career objectives and the means to achieve them.

4. *Placement.* Individuals who wish to enter the labor market are registered, classified occupationally, and referred to prospective employers. Employers submit their needs for workers to the local Employment Service office, and applicants' qualifications are matched to the employers' specifications.

Clients of state employment counselors may be persons who (1) enter the labor market with limited work experience; (2) need information about employment opportunities and their own qualifications; (3) want or need to shift to new or different occupations; (4) experience vocational maladjustment or have personal problems which limit their ability to work. Clients also include older persons seeking to enter or re-enter the labor market and persons who are physically or emotionally handicapped. The Employment Service counselor, in his initial interview with the client, verifies the applicant's need for counseling. If appropriate, counseling is extended in order to (1) identify and delimit the individual's problem in obtaining employment; (2) appraise and analyze his qualifications; (3) provide information about various occupations; (4) determine career plans; and (5) implement such plans through placement.

Many observers have suggested that employment counselors overemphasize placement and relegate counseling to a secondary function, by subordinating the client's personal-social and long-range vocational plans to obtaining immediate job placement.

Mrs. Dorothy McCloud, an Employment Service counselor in the Lafayette, Indiana office, provides the following schedule for a typical day:

A Typical Day as an Employment Service Counselor

Time	Tasks
	Outreach (assigned to other employees).
10 minutes	Intake.
one hour, 10 minutes	Interviewing counselees and routine initial contacts.
three hours	Counseling three to six people per day.
30 minutes	Testing: scheduling, administration, grading, recording.
one hour	Training: selection, referral, and follow-up.
30 minutes	Placement and job development.
10 minutes	Alien immigration.
30 minutes	Management: activities and staff meetings.
10 minutes	Community service.
20 minutes	Career development activities: in-office and out-office training.
seven hours, 30 minutes	Total hours

PREPARATION REQUIRED

The educational requirements for an employment counselor vary from state to state. In general, the minimum educational requirements are a bachelor's degree, preferably with a major area of concentration in one of the social sciences, plus 15 semester hours in counseling or related coursework. Many states have adopted a three-level classification system for counselors. The first level is *employment counselor intern* or *trainee* (minimum qualifications are as stated above). The second level is *employment counselor,* which requires 30 graduate hours in counseling and related courses. The third level is *master counselor,* which requires a master's degree and three years of experience including at least one year in employment counseling.

Many state employment offices have recently organized in-service training programs to upgrade the preparation of new trainees and counselors. Counselors who have a few years of experience with an agency frequently are provided with the financial support to secure additional or advanced training at colleges and universities.

All states require that employment service counselors meet state civil service or merit system requirements. For example, individuals who apply to become trainees are given a written test which covers such areas as vocational guidance, interviewing, occupational testing, the psychology of occupations, and community resources. Candidates for the position of employment counselor (second level) also must pass an examination. The written portion of the examination (about 70 percent) covers techniques of registering, interviewing, placement, vocational guidance, testing, and supervision. The remaining portion of the examination (about 30 percent) involves an evaluation of the applicant's previous experience and training.

WORKING CONDITIONS

State employment counselors have certain hardships to endure, although conditions are improving constantly. In some local employment offices, counselors are reassigned from counseling work at seasonal periods of high unemployment and given the relatively routine tasks of processing unemployment compensation claims. Many local offices do not provide counselors with offices that ensure auditory and visual privacy. In some offices, counselors are expected to conduct as many as 12 to 15 interviews during an eight-hour day, with the result that their work tends to be hurried and superficial.

Most employment counselors work about 40 hours a week and receive various benefits, including vacations, sick leave, pension plans, and insurance coverage.

SALARIES

Beginning salaries for employment counselor trainees are approximately $600 to $750 a month, while those for employment counselors are approximately $630 to $785 a month. Experience and education brings higher salaries. Salaries of highly experienced master counselors may range upwards of $15,000.

CURRENT ISSUES

The use of paraprofessionals (or subprofessionals) is a major issue among employment service counselors, as it is among counselors in other settings. Essentially the issue concerns which tasks should be performed by paraprofessionals and the timing of their intervention. (This issue has been discussed previously in Chapter 1.)

An issue often discussed by employment counselors is whether merely supplying applicants with test or career information data should be referred to as counseling. Many counselors argue that the function of providing occupational information or reporting test data to clients impedes or interrupts the real process of counseling. They argue for separating the two functions by employing specialists in assessment and environmental data as well as persons who wish to engage in personal counseling. Others argue for retaining a counselor who can combine the function of assessment and information collection with that of helping clients to use such information in the counseling relationship.

CAREER PATTERNS

Many employment counselors first are hired essentially as employment interviewers and then later become counselors. They advance through the three-level counselor classification system previously described. Counselors with prior experience often move into administrative and supervisory positions at the local, state, and national levels.

OUTLOOK

Many excellent opportunities are available for employment counselors with the master's degree and prior experience. In addition, new counselors in the field will find many opportunities in federal, state, and local employment service offices.

Recent federal legislation has been enacted which extends services to out-of-school youth, older persons, and disadvantaged individuals and provides training and retraining opportunities for the underemployed and unemployed. The new legislation is expected to be accompanied by an urgent need for additional counselors. In addition to the need for personnel in new and expanded programs, there are extensive replacement demands for counselors leaving the Employment Service.

SOURCES OF FURTHER INFORMATION

Information about requirements for entering Employment Services counseling positions may be obtained from the state civil service or merit system office in each state capital. Professional and governmental organizations which provide materials include:

National Employment Counselor Association
1607 New Hampshire Avenue, N.W.
Washington, D.C. 20009

United States Department of Labor
U.S. Training and Employment Service
Branch of Counseling and Testing Services
Washington, D.C. 20210

Veterans Administration

Since World War II, approximately 12 million veterans have used the educational and rehabilitation benefits available to them through the Veterans Administration. The magnitude of services provided by the Veterans Administration has led some to refer to it as a "quiet giant." It reaches into virtually every geographical area in the nation where people are employed.

The counseling program of the Veterans Administration was established in 1943 in association with programs of vocational rehabilitation, education, and training for veterans. Legal authorization for a veterans counseling service derives from a number of federal laws designed to aid veterans, including Public Law 16, which provided vocational rehabilitation benefits for disabled World War II veterans; Public Law 346, popularly known as the "G.I. Bill" (Public Laws 550 and 894 extended similar benefits to Korean War veterans); Public Law 634, the War Orphans Educational Assistance Act of 1956; and Public Law 89–358, the Veterans

Readjustment Benefits Act of 1966 which provided various VA benefits and services to post-Korean conflict veterans.

The Veterans Administration employs counselors in two different departments, the Department of Veterans Benefits and the Department of Medicine and Surgery. The latter maintains a psychological division which employs over 800 psychologists in approximately 165 VA hospitals and 202 outpatient clinics across the nation. Counselors employed in this department are generally Ph.D.-trained experimental, clinical, and counseling psychologists (numbering approximately 125 to 150) who work in medical settings. The Department of Veterans Benefits employs 800 to 1,000 counselors, maintains 56 regional offices, and contracts for 183 VA Guidance Centers. The latter are located mostly in universities and colleges.

Approximately 350 counselors provide rehabilitation counseling in the Veterans Administration. Originally, counselors employed by the Veterans Administration were called "vocational advisers." Later, the position of "personal counselor" was established, and in 1952 the U.S. Civil Service approved the position of "counseling psychologist."

NATURE OF THE VA COUNSELOR'S WORK

The VA counseling psychologist in the Department of Medicine and Surgery serves as a consultant in all segments of VA health care units. Fundamentally his purpose is to modify maladaptive behavior patterns that interfere with the rehabilitation, restoration, or care of veteran patients. As a psychologist he is involved in therapy, rehabilitation, training, and research functions. A recent innovation in research is the development by VA psychologists of screening procedures for Vietnam veterans which enable vocational and educational counseling services to be provided quickly. The new procedures also shorten the length of hospitalization and lead to fewer readmissions. Currently much attention is being given to developing methods of behavior therapy which promise to reduce the treatment time for a wide spectrum of emotional and physical disorders. In addition, VA psychologists have developed programs for assisting patients suffering from alcoholism, drug addiction, or heavy smoking, as well as a special "reality orientation" training program for geriatric patients.

Counselors employed in the Department of Veterans Benefits provide vocational counseling and educational assistance to (1) veterans and servicemen who completed their service after January 31, 1955; (2) sons and daughters of deceased veterans or of permanently or totally disabled veterans; (3) veterans with service-connected disabilities who wish to pursue a course of training to prepare for suitable occupations; and (4) wives and children of prisoners of war. Eligible veterans are entitled to one month of educational assistance for each month of active duty after January 31, 1955, up to a maximum of 36 months.

Counseling is available for veterans who desire assistance in making vocational choices and in selecting a program of education or training. The counseling model and procedures employed by the Veterans Administration were originally set forth in 1945 in its *Manual of Advisement and Guidance.* Essentially the concepts and practices centered on vocational guidance. Emphasis was placed on the use of occupational information, individual analysis through interviews, review and study of school and work histories, psychological tests for evaluation, and synthesis of data with vocational opportunities and vocational exploration.

In 1951, the published model was modified to combine personal counseling with vocational counseling. The necessity of taking into account the client's perceptions and motivation was stressed. Veterans' counseling records were revised in such a way that fact-finding during the interview was reduced and the importance of the client's attitudes was emphasized. In addition, an attempt was made to stimulate the counselor to formulate tentative hypotheses which would be tested in the counseling relationship.

The Veterans Administration specifies in detail the duties of its counselors. Administrative control is maintained over the size of each counselor's caseload so that the quality of the work will remain high.

Mr. Noble C. Lanier, head of the Veterans Counseling and Training Administration Section of the VA Regional Office in Indianapolis, Indiana, describes a typical day as follows:

A Typical Day as a VA Counselor

7:45–8:00 Arrived at the office early to review schedule for the day. Looks like a busy day with two disabled veterans on the register for initial appointments, a veteran required to have counseling in connection with his second change of program, and an intake interview scheduled with the child of a deceased veteran for early afternoon.

8:00–8:25 Time to dictate a summary of the outcomes of counseling with the wife of a prisoner of war seen yesterday. She appeared grateful for the opportunity to obtain financial assistance to augment her education, but she would willingly exchange the $175 per month to see the safe return of her husband.

8:25–9:30 Joe, a counselee, reported a bit early for his 8:30 appointment. His punctuality may be a desirable indication for future training. He continues to make a favorable impression in the initial interview and appears to have potential in the field of data processing or computer technology. He has thought about this but is relatively uninformed, as are so many who have been attracted by the glamour of these newer occupations. The demands of such a job seems to be compatible with the limitations imposed by his disability: 40% disability for leg and foot wounds caused by an exploding land mine. He needs rehabilitation because he obviously cannot compete with other high school graduates as he has no specialized training or experience. Joe really does not know what he wants or should do. It is mutually agreed that he can profit from a battery of interest, temperament, and aptitude tests, as well as the opportunity to review some of the occupational information in our library. I introduce him to our psychometrist and librarian and inform him that I will see him briefly later on to ensure that our tentative decisions have some support and that we are proceeding in the proper direction.

9:30–9:45 Dictate an analysis of Joe's vocational-educational problems and needs as he views them and include my own appraisal of where we are and what remains to be done.

9:45–10:00 A quick cup of coffee and a breather before a 10:00 appointment. Even at this time, however, there is an opportunity to exchange impressions with colleagues related to current and recent counselees.

10:00–10:30 Back to the office and ready to see Jim. He is late, but this may be understandable since his travel authorization shows that he lives about 80 miles away.

While waiting there is time to review dictation on recent cases and to return a couple of telephone calls. One caller wants information as to how to go about obtaining several hours of college credit through correspondence study and is referred to one of our state universities. Another call is from a technical school instructor wanting to discuss the possibility of readmitting a disabled veteran to their auto mechanics curriculum after having terminated him for excessive absenteeism. We pooled our information and decided it would be desirable for me to see him early next week for a counseling session.

10:30–10:45 Jim still has not reported, and there has been no word from him. A closer inspection of the file suggests that his disability (100%, neuropsychiatric) may be involved. I will have to make a decision of whether to request a follow-up contact at his home by one of our vocational rehabilitation specialists or to refer him to our Vocational Rehabilitation Board for consideration of medical evaluation and follow-up. This action would ensure that all resources—medical, social service, vocational counseling, training, and adjustment—are brought into coordinated action in the rehabilitation of the severely disabled veteran.

10:45–11:00 The morning mail brings, among items relative to VA policies and procedures (which I quickly scan and put aside as irrelevant for the moment), copies of the *Personnel and Guidance Journal,* the *Rehabilitation Record,* and the monthly *Report of the President's Committee on Employment of the Handicapped.* Since Jim has missed his 10:00 appointment I am provided with a relatively rare opportunity to at least scan the articles and mark those of passing interest.

There is also an opportunity to check on Joe and find that his interest pattern is high in computational and clerical preferences. The decision is made to eliminate a mechanical comprehension test and substitute a measure of scholastic aptitude instead. It is noted in his file to consider the possibility of higher level academic training with him.

11:00–11:15 Another counseling psychologist who has had a canceled appointment volunteers to see the veteran who is making a second change of program (I have done the same for my colleagues on similar occasions), and my day eases a bit.

More telephone messages. I return the calls, including one from our office in a distant city seeking information on the offerings of one of our local institutions. This probably indicates that we will soon be asked to accept the transfer of a veteran for training from that office.

11:15–11:45 One of our vocational rehabilitation specialists wants to talk about problems he is having in placing a veteran in job training. We review the file and see factors which do not appear to have been evident during earlier counseling but which have become manifest in the practical reality of getting an employer to give this veteran a chance. It is decided that these may be overcome by taking a different approach, and the vocational rehabilitation specialist agrees to try again. He will include a summary of our discussion and conclusions for future reference in the file.

11:45–12:30 After checking on Joe again and making sure that he understands that his next appointment is a week from today, I am on my way to lunch with three other staff members. As usual, we talk "shop" and find a common understanding of mutual problems.

12:30–1:00 Back at my desk I dictate some routine correspondence and look at the available information concerning a "war orphan" client. Susan's father was killed in action in Korea. She is an only child just turned 18 and recently graduated from high school in the lower third of her class. Apparently she has decided to enter a school of practical nursing after some rather thorough high school counseling. Her high school transcript and an unusually good supplementary letter from her high school counselor are available.

1:00–2:00 Susan arrives accompanied by her mother. She is neatly dressed and rather attractive. After meeting her mother we excuse ourselves and her mother agrees to wait until we have had the opportunity to talk alone. Susan seems to be a mature young lady who has given considerable thought to her vocational choice. She says she knows she is not "bright enough" to go to college and besides she does not think she could afford to go. We review occupational information relative to her chosen objective; she seems quite well informed. We also discuss alternate choices available to her. She has tested her choice to some extent against the alternatives already, and neither of us sees any need for more comprehensive counseling. She has received a letter of acceptance from the school of her choice, a copy of which is placed in her file.

2:00–3:30 Susan's mother is invited to participate at this point. The benefits and details of the Dependents Educational Assistance Program are reviewed and discussed. They seem to be reasonably well informed but are also appreciative of the opportunity to review these matters. The proper forms are completed, and they are on their way. This is representative of many cases of our so-called "intake" counseling, in which there is sufficient advance information to ensure that the proposed course of action is appropriate.

3:30–4:00 Clear desk and check next day's calendar.

PREPARATION REQUIRED

The educational requirements for the U.S. Civil Service position of "counseling psychologist" calls for a doctorate in psychology or counseling, or two years of graduate work with a specified distribution of courses and work experience including therapeutic counseling. Counselors employed in the Department of Medicine and Surgery must have completed 60 graduate hours in counseling or psychology as a minimum. (The doctorate is preferred but is not always required of applicants.)

Qualified individuals for positions in the VA Department of Veterans Benefits have a background of experience and education which enables them to use educational, vocational rehabilitation, or therapeutic counseling techniques to help clients select educational and vocational goals.

Qualifications for counseling positions in the Veterans Administration (except for contracted services) are established by the U.S. Civil Service Commission. Written tests and application forms must be completed by persons who seek such positions. Positions at the federal civil service classification level of GS-11 usually require experience in vocational counseling with either "personal adjustment" counseling or rehabilitation counseling. Positions at the GS-12 grade level usually require experience in all three areas.

WORKING CONDITIONS

Most VA counselors work a 40-hour week with the same federal holidays, vacation periods, and benefits as other civil service divisions. The physical facilities in which they work are usually above-average in quality, but this may vary.

SALARIES

Extensive training and experience bring higher salaries in VA counseling work. Counselor trainees may be employed at the GS-9 level ($10,500). Counselors with 60 semester graduate hours are employed at the GS-11 level (approximately $12,000, depending on the classification step attained within that level). Counselors possessing both the academic requirements as well as three years of experience are usually employed at the GS-12 level ($15,000).

CURRENT ISSUES

Counselors in this setting are confronted with most of the issues previously discussed which relate to counseling in general. However, an issue of particular concern to VA counselors involves the appropriateness of group counseling for clients served by Veterans Benefits counselors. In some regional offices counselors who have established group counseling sessions for their clients, particularly for individuals who seek career and occupational information, report dissatisfaction with the outcomes of such sessions. Their principal objections were that their clients seemed only to need factual information and that many had difficulty in attending regularly scheduled sessions.

Counselors in the Veterans Benefits department currently are extending their services to veterans' wives and widows as well as wives and dependents of prisoners of war. This represents somewhat of a departure from their usual clientele.

CAREER PATTERNS

Career patterns of counselors in the Veterans Administration include specializing in some aspect of assessment, counseling, or disability. Many become supervisors of other counselors.

Some enter administrative positions within regional centers or the national agency.

OUTLOOK

The Veterans Administration is one of the few counseling agencies that does not have a shortage of counselors. It has little difficulty in recruiting counselors. In 1971, funds for expanding counseling positions were made available which should lead to some openings in the program.

SOURCES OF FURTHER INFORMATION

The most direct source is the Civil Service Commission. The address and forms required are available from the local post offices for use in applying for civil service positions.

Programs for the Disadvantaged

Federal legislation supporting the establishment of counseling services along with other types of assistance in a variety of settings has proliferated during the past few years. This legislation not only has heightened the demand for counselors but also has identified specific target populations that may benefit from counseling services. Much recent legislation has been aimed at segments of the population commonly referred to as culturally different or culturally unassimilated. Terms such as "chronically poor," "poverty-stricken," and "socially and culturally disadvantaged" have been employed to describe individuals handicapped by depressed social and economic conditions.

The range of these federally supported counseling services is extremely broad. Authority for many of the programs was given originally to the Department of Labor, but subsequent legislation or executive decree has shifted some programs to other federal departments and offices, principally the Department of Health, Education, and Welfare.

Four major federal laws are the source of authority for many such programs. The Vocational Education Act, as amended, provides for vocational counseling for people who are out of school and seeking employment. This is currently a highly critical area, for unemployment rates among youth have risen greatly. During the decade of the 1960's several pieces of federal legislation have stimulated growth in the area. The Manpower Development and Training Act, as amended, provides for counseling in connection with occupational training and retraining of large numbers of unemployed workers. The Economic Opportunity Act, as amended, provides for counseling to implement programs such as Job Corps, Neighborhood Youth Corps, Work Training, Work Experience, and Urban and Rural Community Action. The Social Security Act, as amended, established the Work Incentive program.

Many have pointed out that the word "disadvantaged" conveys inadequacy and fails to present a well-rounded picture of the individual's culture, by ignoring his strengths while emphasizing his weaknesses. That there is considerable resentment among persons labeled as "disadvantaged" has been well documented.

NATURE OF THE COUNSELOR'S WORK IN PROGRAMS FOR THE DISADVANTAGED

Central to these programs has been the employment of counselors whose goals have been expressed by Edward Gross, a sociologist, as follows: (1) to increase the accuracy of the individual's self-concept; (2) to increase the accuracy of the individual's environmental perceptions; (3) to integrate the individual's self-concept with environmental realities; (4) to present relevant information; and (5) to improve the individual's ability to make and execute plans.[4] An important goal which should be added to this list is that of referring individuals to a job or training program.

Essentially, counselors employed in programs aimed at the disadvantaged seek to help their clients modify self-defeating attitudes and to cope with unduly limited job opportunities. While part of their work involves individual and group counseling, a substantial portion is devoted to modifying the attitudes of persons who employ, supervise, and work with the disadvantaged. The counselor's relationships with his clients are influenced by such forces as the welfare system, the schools, medical delivery systems, work opportunities, and the family structure to which the client belongs. While similarities exist, radical differences are present in the problems of disadvantaged Negroes, Indians, Appalachian whites,

[4] Edward Gross, "Counselors Under Fire: Youth Opportunity Centers," *Personnel and Guidance Journal,* Vol. 47 (January 1969), p. 405.

Puerto Ricans, and Mexican Americans. Persons who work with these subgroups must take into account the social, cultural, psychological, and historical factors which influence each individual member's present status.

Experience in programs conducted in many different types of settings seems to indicate that traditional counseling techniques focusing on the individual are not sufficient. Combinations of counseling and outreach work in the community and with the individual family seem to produce better outcomes.

PREPARATION REQUIRED

As in other settings, counselors with extensive training who have earned the master's degree or Ph.D. in counseling, psychology, rehabilitation, or social work are preferred. Specialized preparation for counseling work in these diverse settings has not been formally established by any agency or professional organization. Many agencies prefer to employ counselors whose social, ethnic, or racial backgrounds are similar to those of the clientele served.

WORKING CONDITIONS

Counselors in programs for the disadvantaged work in a wide range of physical settings: storefront buildings, homes, city or county owned or leased buildings, apartment and office buildings, etc. Their workdays tend to be long and are geared to the time when their clients are most accessible.

Usually counselors are employed by a local agency under contract to the federal government authority that is responsible for a particular program. Counseling positions as such often terminate when the contract is ended. This gives rise to much job uncertainty and undoubtedly contributes to the high turnover of counseling personnel in such positions.

SALARIES

Salary figures are difficult to establish. Most positions filled by professionals offer salaries competitive with other settings. Often salaries are slightly inflated due to the somewhat tenuous nature of government contracts.

CURRENT ISSUES

An issue of considerable magnitude is whether counseling services for the disadvantaged can be justified. Edward Gross has concluded that many assumptions about the work of the counselor are untenable: that clients come voluntarily to the counselor; that clients want help; that the disadvantaged client is viewed by the counselor as an individual rather than as a case. He believes that these implicit assumptions, pervasive in all forms of counseling, cannot exist in counseling work with disadvantaged clients because of the bureaucratic conditions present in government programs, the poverty and demoralization of clients, and the problem of race. He has suggested that highly directive counseling is perhaps more appropriate for the population and further, that a self-help group approach which builds upon the client's informal community structure (unorganized neighborhood activities) would be even better.[5]

CAREER PATTERNS

The career patterns of counselors in programs for the disadvantaged are largely unknown because of the recent emergence of this area of counseling. Some counselors, once a program contract is terminated, move to other funded programs to serve as counselors, supervisors of counselors, or administrators of the program.

OUTLOOK

If federal monies continue to be made available, positions will open for urgently needed counselors in this setting. At the present time it is difficult to project the degree to which government intervention and activity will continue to support such programs.

SOURCES OF FURTHER INFORMATION

Vocational Education Division
Office of Education
Department of Health, Education, and Welfare
Washington, D.C. 25001

Manpower Development and Training
Department of Labor
Washington, D.C. 20212

Economic Opportunity Office
Department of Health, Education, and Welfare
Washington, D.C. 25001

[5] Ibid., pp. 404–409.

Social Security Administration
Department of Health, Education, and Welfare
Washington, D.C. 25001

Correctional and Penal Institutions

Finding the means to reshape the attitudes and behaviors of delinquents has been an unending quest. Many penal authorities responsible for administering reformatories and prisons have called for experimental and innovative approaches to make the prison sentence into a constructive, rehabilitative experience. That past and present approaches fall short has been well documented by the high rate of recidivism found in most correctional institutions.

Contemporary thought on treatment procedures and processes has moved well beyond the paralyzing attitudes of retribution and punishment and now advocates approaches directed toward changing human behavior through casework, counseling, therapy, and education. Unfortunately, actual practice lags far behind. The penal system in this country at the federal, state, and local levels employs relatively few professionally prepared treatment personnel in comparison to the population served.

Social casework, clinical psychology, and psychiatry are the helping professions usually involved in the federal and state prisons and reformatories. It is estimated that about 1,200 social workers, psychologists, and psychiatrists are employed in state and federal adult prisons who are responsible for the diagnosis and treatment of over 201,000 prisoners. There are about 17,000 employees in public institutions for juvenile delinquents, with slightly over 60 percent classified as staffing educational or treatment services. In addition there are about 13,000 persons classified as probation and parole officers. The number of counselors as such who work in the state and federal institutions is unknown.

NATURE OF THE CORRECTIONAL COUNSELOR'S WORK

The two major tasks performed by social workers and counselors are analysis and counseling. The "classification" or treatment plan for each inmate is based, in theory if not in practice, on gathering data about the inmate's life history from the individual and from outside social agencies that have served him and his family. Beyond the usual diagnostic objective of ascertaining the deficits and strengths of the individual, analysis of such data seeks to provide an understanding of the past, present, and probable future interaction of the prisoner in society. In short, information is gathered which helps to define the correctional problem of the client and which frequently includes interviewing and administration of psychological tests.

Both individual and group counseling is conducted in such matters as the problems and situations experienced by the inmate. Group counseling is being used increasingly to encourage inmates to discuss their situations; to vent any suppressed hostilities toward society, authority, families, or other inmates; and to gain insight into the causes of their problems and how to modify them. Group counseling seems particularly useful in helping inmates learn to accept the rights of others to their own opinions and beliefs. It also provides inmates with the opportunity to experience helping others who need it.

Counselors who serve in correctional positions, which include probation and parole officers, seek to assist adult and juvenile offenders on probation or parole in adjusting to society. In some cases, they investigate the life history and background of individuals who are under the jurisdiction of the court. Their reports assist the judge in making his decisions about the individual. They counsel persons who are on parole or probation, help them secure necessary training or education, or assist them to enter the labor market and to use the resources available to them in the community. Many offenders have marital or family problems that need to be dealt with in counseling.

Steve Poland, who is employed at Pine Hills School in Miles City, Montana, has this to say about the school and its treatment staff:

> . . . let me tell you about Pine Hills School for Boys. It is a juvenile institution. Any male between 10 and 18 years of age can be sent here by a judge. The offense can be anything from truancy to murder. Most students are here for truancy, theft (car), burglary, etc. There is no minimum or maximum time established. The school staff decides when to release a student. They can retain him until he is 21 years old; upon release he is placed in aftercare. This is similar to parole, except most aftercare workers have a background in social work. They take more of a counseling

approach than do most parole officers. Aftercare decides when to discharge him, but they must do so when he is 21 years old. We presently have around 90 students. During the school year our population will increase to around 150. The state legislature has limited our population to 120. There are no walls or fences. The students are pretty much given free movement. They are locked in the residence halls at night. Although there are some work details, most of the students are enrolled either in the ungraded elementary school or the secondary school. Both are accredited, and the secondary school students compete in inter-high school athletic events. The classes are small, usually about eight students. All teachers are certified to teach.

Our treatment staff consists of a Director of Clinical Services, Assistant Director, two psychologists, six caseworkers (two openings now), a half-time psychiatrist, a chaplain with a counseling orientation. The Director has a M.S.W., the Assistant Director has a B.A. in social work, one psychologist has a B.A. in psychology, and the other (me) has a Ph.D. in counseling. The caseworkers have B.A. degrees, most of which are in social work. They have some routine functions, but with the small caseload they have time for counseling. The routine duties include checking the client's incoming and outgoing mail, arranging home leaves, planning family visits, correspondence with aftercare, etc. A federal grant provides money for family therapy sessions. The student's parents come here, or the counselor and student go to his home for family therapy sessions. The program looks good. Vocational Rehabilitation provides money for correction of physical disabilities (tattoo removal, eyeglasses, etc.).

Mike Strouf, also employed at Pine Hills School as a caseworker, has supplied the following outline of a typical day as a correctional counselor in that school.

A Typical Day as a Correctional Counselor

8:00–9:00	Open mail, organize day's appointments; receive two telephone calls regarding placement of two boys; conference with house parents.
9:00–10:00	Counseling boy regarding violation of parole and his subsequent return. Received two telephone calls regarding medical attention for boys.
10:00–11:00	Counseling boy in regard to placement.
11:00–12:00	Counseling boy regarding housing unit problems.

	Telephone calls to follow-up boys who were released.
12:00–1:00	Lunch.
1:00–2:00	Correspondence to aftercare personnel; paperwork and reports in respect to vocational placements.
2:00–3:00	Counseling boy regarding lack of vocational placement.
3:00–4:00	Counseling boy with family conflicts and Indian identification.
4:00–5:00	Counseling boy regarding housing unit behavior.

PREPARATION REQUIRED

Specifications for the educational preparation of counselors in the correctional system vary greatly from state to state. A large number of counselors currently employed have had little graduate preparation for their positions. Individuals who have a master's degree in counseling, social work, psychology, or behavioral science are preferred, but the demand for educational and treatment personnel has exceeded the supply. Most professionals are required to meet civil service or merit system requirements.

WORKING CONDITIONS

Permanent appointees usually work for a probationary period of six months or one year. Most counselors are assigned heavy caseloads. Inmates in many institutions are often available for only an hour or so during the mornings and afternoons because a large amount of their time is devoted to institutional routine. Counselors, as other professional workers employed in prisons, are not immune to coming under the environmental influence of the prison, which can lead to becoming indifferent, frustrated, or demoralized. Most settings provide fringe benefits such as paid vacations, sick leave, retirement plans, and insurance coverage.

SALARIES

Salaries of professionals in state prisons and correctional institutions are usually a good bit lower than they are in other work settings. Annual beginning salaries are estimated at $6,000 to $7,000 for counselors employed in these settings. It should be kept in mind that many do not have extensive professional training or graduate degrees. Salaries of supervisors of counselors range from $8,000 to $12,000. Salaries are generally reviewed annually.

CURRENT ISSUES

An issue often discussed concerns whether penal and correctional institutions should employ a large number of professionals, i.e., those who have extensive advanced graduate training, to work directly with inmates. Many authorities advocate employing fewer professionals—but a larger number than at present—to work with technical or custodial staff members (guards, orderlies, work supervisors, house parents, recreational leaders) in order to improve their relationships with inmates. These authorities argue that professionals have such limited direct contact with imprisoned individuals that their ability to effect change directly is negligible. Others assert that professionals are needed in order to provide highly specialized services directly to the inmates, whose individual needs and situations are severe and vary greatly. Because of these differences of opinion treatment plans must be individually determined. This issue, of course, exists in other settings due to the existing personnel shortages and the desire to reach the maximum number of persons in the most effective way.

CAREER PATTERNS

Very little is known about the career patterns of counselors who serve in correctional and penal institutions. Many observers are of the opinion that counselors who work in such settings are considerably less mobile in their work than professionals in other settings.

OUTLOOK

Employment opportunities for counselors in positions associated with correctional and penal institutions and courts are expected to be excellent during the 1970's. The demand for manpower in these settings is expected to outstrip the supply, particularly for counselors prepared at the graduate level. Federal funds have been provided by the Correctional Rehabilitation Study Act of 1965 to study systematically manpower needs and resources in the area, to determine educational and in-service training needs, and to recruit personnel. This act has served as a stimulant to progress in the field.

SOURCES OF FURTHER INFORMATION

Bureau of Prisons
U.S. Department of Justice
Washington, D.C. 20537

Administrative Office of the U.S. Courts
Supreme Court Building
Washington, D.C. 20544

National Council on Crime and Delinquency
44 East 23rd Street
New York, New York 10010

United States Board of Parole
U.S. Department of Justice
Washington, D.C. 20537

Community Mental Health Clinics

The expansion of counseling services in educational settings has been paralleled during the past decade by support for similar services among state, county, and municipal governments as well as in the voluntary and private sectors of our society. Community agencies that offer counseling services differ according to types of services offered, client population served, problems treated, and source of financial support. Many community agencies are supported by tax funds and are under the administration of government agencies. Others are supported by taxes, community philanthropic organizations, client fees, and various combinations of such funding sources.

NATURE OF THE COMMUNITY CLINIC COUNSELOR'S WORK

Many communities have established community mental health clinics which offer assistance directly to children, adolescents, and adults. Community mental health centers seek to make available several forms of care: individual and group therapy, day-care programs, inpatient care, half-way houses, emergency or "walk-in" services for the disturbed individual. Continuity of care and easy transfer from one service unit to another is stressed. These services are directed toward helping the individual and the social system of which he is a member to function together as harmoniously as possible.

It has been well documented that thousands of children are neglected, suffer emotional disorders, and live in destructive poverty. Much is known about why abnormal development occurs in children as well as adults; however there are relatively few answers as to what can be done to prevent or treat individuals for whom things have gone wrong. It is known, for example, that preventive measures are essential and most effective if available in the early years of life. It is also generally agreed that childhood is a critical stage of development—one which, if neglected or mishandled, can result in irreversible psychological damage.

Many children and youth, including those who are emotionally disturbed, mentally ill, mentally retarded, handicapped, or delinquent are not receiving care and treatment through facilities appropriate to their needs and through which they could be kept within a normal community setting. Many children remain untreated because community mental health services are either nonexistent, fragmented, or inconveniently located. Current estimates indicate that only about one-third of our children and youth in serious need of attention receive appropriate service, care, and treatment.

Basic to a comprehensive philosophy regarding the community mental health center is the belief that mental disorder is not the private misery of the individual or a personal problem solely of his own making. Emotional disorders are rooted as well as manifest in the social relationships and cultural background of the individual. To eliminate human distress and to enhance human and social potential at all ages are targets for comprehensive mental health centers. These objectives were given a tremendous impetus by legislation in the early to mid-1960's which provided federal funding for construction and staffing of facilities for the delivery of services. Federal, state, and local funds have been combined to provide basic services for the disturbed and retarded. This legislation has led to the establishment of literally hundreds of totally new agencies and combinations of existing agencies and services to provide comprehensive mental health care at the community level.

Existing community mental health centers seek to assist individuals and families in gaining the emotional and economic support they need. Fundamental services offered in such programs include (1) basic prevention of emotional disorder through, for example, attending to the need for adequate housing, neighborhood improvement, and the dietary well-being of children; (2) remedial care for persons with symptoms of a complex emotional problem; and (3) tertiary care, within the community, for the more seriously disturbed. Today's comprehensive mental health clinic works within the local community to extend its outreach efforts, to identify persons in need and deliver services to them, and to conduct broad public educational programs in mental health. Outpatient services and residential care services are being made available in many communities for the immediate treatment of individuals.

Counselors in comprehensive mental health clinics are involved in outreach and education programs, as well as the delivery of direct services of a remedial nature to persons who suffer from emotional disorders arising from faulty training, unhappy life experiences, situational conflicts, difficulties with school, sex, or siblings, and child-parent relations.

Counselors have been employed in some community clinics to conduct group programs which provide corrective emotional experiences for persons who, as the result of a disadvantaged environment, experience apathy, hopelessness, and alienation. They have sought to help these individuals to develop a new picture of their ability to be useful, active, and effective by building on the healthy components of each individual's personality.

The traditional combination of psychiatrists, clinical psychologists, and social workers on the staff of mental health clinics is currently undergoing changes not only in the number and kinds of professionals and paraprofessionals employed but also in tasks performed. More broadly based interdisciplinary teams, composed of professionals grounded in the dynamics and techniques of individual treatment and group procedures, are expected to conduct diagnostic and therapeutic functions as well as supervise paraprofessionals. In addition the team will treat not only the individual and his family but also the community by restructuring the environment of the family and neighborhood.

Charles R. Fisher, a staff psychologist at Arapahoe Mental Health Center (near Denver, Colorado), presents a typical day in his work schedule. He functions primarily as a consultant to the public schools.

The following represents a relatively heavy day's schedule in a high school of 2,500 students, grades 10–12, with a counseling department of seven people. The school emphasizes college preparatory programs in an open-campus concept. The counselor-mental health consultant may devote approximately eight to 16 hours per week to a particular school.

A Typical Day as a Mental Health Consultant to Schools

8:00–9:00 Individual or group consultation with counselors, teachers, and administrators. This generally results in one of three decisions:

(1) Consult with the referring professional as to possible dispositions and directions for him to choose from in handling the case.
(2) Agree to see the professional's client for one interview to verify his perceptions of the case.
(3) Interview the student's parents with the referring professional and with or without the student present but at least with the student's awareness and permission beforehand.

9:00–11:00 Individual appointments with students for single interview evaluations resulting in:

(1) Formulating case disposition feedback to referring professional, or
(2) Contracting with the client for a series of four to six sessions.
(3) Individual referral to the Community Mental Health Center with parental permission (if under 18).
(4) Continued evaluative interviews with parents or family.

11:00–12:00 Serving as co-facilitator with a counselor in a regular counseling group of teachers or counselors.

1:00–2:00 This time may be used for one of the following activities: (1) Conducting a "Drop-in rap group" with students having free time at that hour; (2) making a classroom visit to (*a*) acquaint students and teachers with the services available to students and families, or (*b*) have discussion sessions in classes concerning mental hygiene and personal growth issues; (3) conducting (with counselors) a "parents' worry clinic" mainly for mothers of adolescents in the school, focusing on issues of concern to them in dealing with adolescents at home and in school. This clinic usually is held twice a month and often requires two hours.

2:00–3:00 Consult with personnel involved in the Behavior Modification Truancy Program and the Positive Reinforcement Through Academic Contracts Program.

3:00–5:00 Individual, family, or group therapeutic intervention at the Mental Health Center, generally with cases I have referred.

One evening a week is devoted to a 1½-hour "multiple-family group" in the school, which I conduct jointly with a second consultant and two counselors for families who have been referred to the group by the consultant for a series of six sessions in the group. The group consists of four families, and the model is regular family therapy conducted in a multiple-family group setting.

PREPARATION REQUIRED

Traditionally the staff of mental health clinics has consisted almost exclusively of a team composed of a psychiatrist, clinical psychologist, and psychiatric social worker. Contemporary views of broadened services have led to staffing patterns which now include a wide variety of allied professions. For example, community-based responsive programs now employ individuals who provide a much wider variety of services, including educational consultants, counseling psychologists, teachers for the emotionally disturbed, research personnel, as well as consulting personnel whose specialties can include such fields as community psychology, sociology, and urban planning. Services usually include not only direct treatment of patients but also an examination of the impact of the environment on the individual who seeks assistance.

The trend toward diversity of personnel in mental health clinics creates a situation in which an adequate description of the required education and training of counselors is made almost impossible. (Information regarding the traditional mental health positions is available in the sources of information listed at the end of this section.) However, the newer positions often represent hybrid occupations or professions that are currently being created, defined, and modified.

Few professionals in mental health centers, whether of the traditional or emerging variety, have less than a master's degree. The vast majority have had training in psychology or social work beyond the master's degree, plus considerable experience.

WORKING CONDITIONS

The physical facilities available to workers in this field vary from excellent to poor. Many new buildings have been constructed, but outdated facilities are still common. It is important to note that the work in this field is conducted in settings ranging from storefront clinics to brand new multipurpose physical plants.

Personnel shortages have tended to mean heavy caseloads and long working hours. Office hours must be flexible in order to encourage maximum use of services by the public. Evening and weekend hours are not uncommon.

SALARIES

Pay scales, generally good because of the demand for personnel, are usually better than those for similar personnel in state agencies and school settings. A beginning (doctorate level) psychologist's annual salary ranges between $13,000 and $16,000. Salaries for two-year master's degree social workers, rehabilitation counselors, and other subdoctoral personnel usually fall within the range of $8,500 to $12,000. Psychiatrists' salaries not uncommonly begin at the $30,000 level and fairly often exceed $40,000 per year, depending on their field of specialization and the amount of administrative responsibility assigned to them.

CURRENT ISSUES

An issue of considerable importance involves the funding of mental health programs. Comprehensive mental health care attempts to provide service to a greatly enlarged segment of the population. It attempts to make assistance available to population subgroups who do not have the financial means to pay for it. While some expansion has occurred in private and group insurance benefits and in Medicare and Medicaid programs, such benefits are still inadequate or unavailable to a relatively large portion of the population. The initial windfall of federal financing in the 1960's has already been seriously curtailed. Construction and staffing funds for comprehensive mental health centers now rely heavily on state and local resources. This has occurred at a time when local government as well as local philanthropic sources are deeply concerned about financing public activities such as education, welfare, and public housing.

Another issue involves the redefinition and restructuring of the delivery of mental health services. In many ways this issue parallels that existing in the field of medicine and involves the question of increasing costs, availability of personnel, and accessibility of services. Another element which has rarely achieved adequate implementation in the medical field involves preventive activities in mental health. The field of community mental health today focuses on prevention through active intervention in the aspects of community life which create mental health problems. This intervention can range from active efforts to improve slum areas to stimulation, through education, of public concern for the almost endless list of necessary specialized services directed toward alleviating mental health problems.

CAREER PATTERNS

The typical career pattern seems to involve several years of experience in a mental health occupation, followed by advancement to a supervisory or administrative position. Many professionals make parallel moves to larger mental health centers that may provide an opportunity for specialization, research, supervisory responsibility, or entry into an administrative position.

OUTLOOK

During the past decade, growth in this field has been phenomenal. The opportunities for the 1970's appear good, if funding problems are solved and recent gains can be consolidated and advanced.

SOURCES OF FURTHER INFORMATION

National Institute of Mental Health
Division of Manpower and Training Programs
5454 Wisconsin Avenue
Chevy Chase, Maryland 20015

Director, Division of Mental Health
State Board of Health
(Capital city, State)

Summary

In the various settings discussed in this chapter, counselors enter the field from a wide variety of backgrounds. This occurs largely because the counseling occupations within educational institutions (described in Chapter 3) tend to have highly structured certification requirements and related educational requirements, while the career opportunities in government offer a more flexible alternative. It should also be noted that preparation for employment in educational settings does not hinder one from entering the areas of counseling described in this chapter.

Counselors choose to enter the positions described in this chapter, in all probability, because of a desire to work with a particular type of clientele, such as the handicapped worker or the veteran. Despite the apparent differences in background and employment setting, a great deal of similarity exists among individuals offering personal assistance to others, whether in educational or government settings.

CAREER COUNSELING OPPORTUNITIES IN OTHER SETTINGS

CHAPTER 5

The material in this chapter describes counseling services conducted in various settings. Because of the variety and, at least in some cases, the relatively small number of counselors involved, the previous format (i.e., nature of work, preparation, salaries, etc.) employed in earlier chapters is not used in the following presentation.

Community-Based Programs

FAMILY SERVICE AGENCIES

About 340 or more accredited, nonprofit family-serving agencies across the nation provide counseling services to help individuals and families who experience conflict and stress. The national parent organization of these agencies, the Family Service Association of America, was established in 1911. The association sets professional standards, provides consultant services, and accredits local Family Service agencies. In addition, it publishes a journal, *Social Casework*, and directs pilot programs related to mental health, the aged, the family, and community problems.

Most local family service agencies are financed by community funds or by various church-related groups and by client fees (based on ability to pay). Each local agency's policies are established by a board of directors composed of community leaders.

Typical client concerns include marital problems, parent-child conflicts, personal adjustment, pre-marriage planning, unwed parenthood, debt and budget management. During a recent period (approximately one year) an agency in Lafayette, Indiana, staffed by five professionals, reported that 536 families received service (396 women, 259 men, and 75 children, for a total of 730 family members). During the same period the agency staff attended 170 community meetings, conducted five family-life education programs in the community, and presented two educational plays or skits dramatizing family situations. Approximately half of their clients were self-referrals, and the remainder came from sources such as public welfare officials, clergy, physicians, attorneys, school personnel, police, employers, etc. This agency focused its services on the following types of situations:

marital problems, 252 cases

parent-child behavior, 85 cases

family relationships, 48 cases

personal adjustment, 82 cases

situational or environmental problems, 37 cases

financial problems, 24 cases

other (unclassified), 7 cases

Across the country, some 4,500 counselors, primarily social caseworkers, are employed in family service agencies. Recommended starting salaries for family service counselors are approximately $10,000 for those with a master's degree in social work (two-year graduate degree). Career patterns for them are similar to those of other counselors: after some experience, they pursue a specialty in casework, administration, supervision, or research. Some go into private practice, generally in association with a psychiatrist or a group of other professionals.

All accredited family service agencies maintain family counseling services and seek to improve community conditions influencing family life. Some local agencies conduct child adoption and foster care programs, homemaker services, and vocational counseling. The Family Service Association estimates that family agencies are geographically available to 63 percent of the population of the United States and 33 percent of the population of Canada. The association also indicates that a growing crisis in services exists because of inadequate financing, staff shortages, and increasing numbers of people seeking help.

SOURCES OF FURTHER INFORMATION

Further information about counseling in family service agencies may be obtained from:

Family Service Association of America
44 East 23rd Street
New York, New York 10010

CHILD GUIDANCE CLINICS

The work of child guidance clinics is similar, in many ways, to child services included in community mental health clinics (see Chapter 4). Therefore, consideration here is limited to a few remarks about the nature of the clientele served in order to call attention to child guidance clinics as a setting where counseling takes place.

Many communities maintain child guidance clinics staffed by psychologists, social workers, and consulting psychiatrists. Children who are referred to child guidance clinics usually display troublesome personality traits or intractable behavior —often symptoms of serious underlying disturbances. Maladjustment, especially in young children, may be indicated, for example, by chronic thumb-sucking, nail-biting, masturbation, enuresis, night terrors, and the like. Or it may be highlighted by personality traits such as extreme sensitiveness, seclusiveness, apathy, anxiety, fantasy, moodiness, or obstinacy.

Generally, child guidance centers treat children between the ages of three and 16. Mental retardation or chronic neurological and pathological states such as epilepsy or childhood schizophrenia are not treated by the child guidance clinic. Most clinics involve the child and the parents in treatment. Some communities have established traveling child guidance clinics with branch offices to serve sparsely settled or rural areas. Often teams from the central office are assisted by local health and welfare agencies.

JEWISH VOCATIONAL SERVICE

B'nai B'rith is a social and philanthropic organization which opened a Vocational Service Bureau in Washington, D.C. in

1938. Presently it operates vocational service programs in 20 large cities under the title of Jewish Vocational Services. The national headquarters office conducts vocational guidance research and group counseling services. Moreover, the Bureau has engaged for a number of years in extensive publication and distribution of high-quality materials providing occupational information.

Approximately 30 counselors are currently employed in the 20 local agencies, almost all of whom have the master's degree or preparation beyond that level. In each agency the director serves full time, and in the larger centers (New York, Washington, Chicago, etc.) most counselors are also employed full time. While clients come from all age groups, including adults seeking to change occupations or to re-enter the labor market, the majority of their clients fall within the adolescent age group. Clients are referred from schools, friends, rabbis.

Counselors in the Vocational Service Bureau make use of workshops and other large and small group approaches, in addition to counseling, to evaluate client personalities and to help them in vocational planning.

URBAN LEAGUE

Some local branches of the Urban League employ counselors primarily to help persons handicapped by economic or social difficulties or who have experienced discriminatory practices in their work. In many local Urban League offices, counselors conduct initial interviews and then refer clients to community agencies that offer specialized services appropriate to the client's needs.

Marriage Counseling

Marriage counseling is a specialty engaged in by an increasing number of helping professionals. Educational preparation frequently is in clinical psychology, sociology, social psychology, or social casework and incorporates a clinical internship focusing on marriage problems. Marriage counselors have established a professional organization, the American Association of Marriage and Family Counselors, which now has approximately 1,000 members.

Many authorities report that the public's demand for marriage counseling has grown increasingly in recent years. They trace its need to (1) ignorance and misinformation about love, marriage, sex, and child-rearing practices; (2) shifts away from the traditional authoritarian husband-father figure and the extended family; (3) changing sexual mores; and (4) modifications in character engendered by the public media, such as films, television, and newspapers. These factors are often cited as having a pervasive influence on many marriages, causing increased misunderstanding, tension, conflict, and lack of communication. Large numbers of couples, feeling uncertain about their marriage, increasingly are seeking professional help.

Among its goals, marriage counseling seeks to resolve tension-producing difficulties, to repair the communication breakdown that often occurs between husband and wife or among family members, to facilitate understanding of the marriage or family relationships, and to promote their clients' understanding of and functioning within the marriage. Marital maladjustment is viewed primarily, but not exclusively, as a psychological maladjustment of one or both partners. Marriage counseling provides the conditions and impetus by which clients communicate their feelings and experiences and seek optimal development of their potentialities.

The American Association of Marriage Counselors has established professional standards for membership. A basic requirement is the master's degree in social casework (two graduate years) or the doctoral degree or its equivalent in training and experience in the fields of human development, psychology, sociology, medicine, or law. Additionally, five years of experience in marriage counseling is necessary for "active" membership and three years for "associate" membership. Students in professional preparation programs are eligible for "associate-in-training" status. A "fellow" classification is available for those who have held active membership for five years and who have made a contribution to the field. Not all practicing marriage counselors are able to meet these standards. However, several states have passed legislation which regulates the certification or licensing of marriage counselors, and a number of states are currently considering such laws.

The broad range of problems treated by the marriage counselor includes: entering marriage, making the marriage work, obtaining a divorce, sexual problems, concerns about appropriate masculine roles (functioning as a person, husband, lover, father) or appropriate feminine role (functioning as an individual, wife, lover, mother). In most marriage counseling cases, both the husband and wife, and frequently all family members, are counseled, as working with one marriage partner alone often merely serves to widen the breach in the relationship.

Attorneys, clergymen, and physicians are particularly active in referring couples who need pre- or post-marital counseling. In some situations, supplying factual information (for example, in regard to sexual matters, family planning, budgeting) is all that may be needed. Other situations call for counseling or short-term psychotherapy that seeks to facilitate a better understanding of oneself, the partner, and the relationship. In providing assistance, the marriage counselor must attend not only to the psychological make-up of each partner but also to the sociopsychological factors involved. He must concentrate on the interaction that exists between husband and wife and the nature of the relationship they have established or seek to establish.

The promotion and preservation of marriages are not necessarily the primary goals of marriage counselors. In many cases it is true that marriage counselors seek to develop, maintain, or restore marriages; however, in some situations, particularly if the clients have made a mutually agreeable decision to dissolve an unsatisfactory marriage, counselors aid clients to live without the partner and to develop relationships with others.

Marriage counselors are employed in public and private clinics or engage in independent practice. Many clinics and private offices of marriage counselors are located in large cities and near universities. In 1962, the American Association of Marriage Counselors adopted an ethical code that set forth behavioral standards regarding such areas as advertising, confidential information, fees, and referrals.

SOURCES OF FURTHER INFORMATION

American Association of Marriage Counselors, Inc.
3603 Lemmon Avenue
Dallas, Texas 75219

National Council on Family Relations
1219 University Avenue, S.E.
Minneapolis, Minn. 55444

Business and Industrial Personnel Settings

In our society most people who work full time spend approximately half of their waking hours on the job. Work experience for many also means membership in an organization, subjection to the complexities and demands of organizational life, and numerous conflict situations.

The origin of counseling programs in business and industrial settings is usually attributed to the Western Electric Company in Chicago, where studies were begun to determine the relation of production to working conditions and environment. Currently, many business and industrial organizations employ counselors and psychologists in their personnel departments in order to facilitate human relations and good mental health among employees. Businesses employ counselors for these ends not merely because it is humanitarian or good for public relations, but because employee behavior that is indicative of poor mental health is not personally desirable or economically productive for the company.

Employees whose personal problems interfere with their work are referred to counselors employed by the company for individual counseling or screened by such counselors for referral to private or public agencies. The work of the counselor or psychologist in the industrial setting often includes (1) conducting human relations training for management and supervisory personnel; (2) evaluating individuals for employment in supervisory, management, and executive positions; (3) initiating programs that will alleviate or prevent absenteeism, accidents, alcoholism, and pilferage; and (4) referring employees with serious disturbances that require long term psychotherapy to the appropriate agencies and practitioners.

Numerous surveys of companies employing counselors reveal that few businesses have full-time counselors (presumably less than 10 percent). Some companies, however, employ such professionals on a part-time or consulting basis.

Adult Education Programs

Adults are going back to school in record-breaking numbers. Thousands of adults increasingly find their jobs changing so radically that they require further education or training in order to cope with the demands of their present position or to re-enter the labor market in a different capacity. Adults return to school not only for vocational reasons but also to learn more about their culture and to improve themselves.

Adult education programs are offered by many high schools, junior or community colleges, universities, and industries. These programs have broad objectives ranging from initial training through retraining for new jobs, often including general cultural improvement as well as activities focusing on handicrafts, hobbies, etc. In short, programs range from specific skill training for new and different jobs to recreational programs. Some of these programs employ counselors to help adults select specific courses appropriate to their interests and their future goals. Many individuals desperately need someone to talk with who can appreciate their troubled feelings and accept their frustrations and uncertainties without condemnation. Often the counseling experience helps them to achieve personal and vocational goals or to adjust to their existing situation. Clients who particularly may need the counselor's services include high school dropouts, women who are entering or re-entering the labor market, and men and women who enroll to further their general cultural and intellectual knowledge.

Counselors who work in this setting often feel inadequately prepared if their counseling practicum or internship experience was exclusively with high school and college students. Many counseling tools and tests are inappropriate or of limited value because they were developed for student groups. Counselors face a considerable challenge in adult education programs where interest and motivation often are more important than appraised skills and abilities.

Pastoral Counseling

The term *pastoral work* was originally used by ministers to refer to their spiritual responsibility for the congregation. Increased demands on ministers to deal with the personal concerns of individuals led to a recognition that the average minister was insufficiently prepared to deal with the range and intensity of problems presented to him. Such demands frequently include many concerns other than spiritual matters. Currently many ministerial associations, church organizations, community associations of churches, and individual churches have established especially designed counseling services for their parishioners and others who seek help. Many of these centers accept as clients any community resident, but some restrict extended services to church members who support the service financially. Some centers employ trained counselors and ministers on a part-time basis, while others are staffed entirely by ministers, many of whom have had some training in counseling. Such centers often contract for psychiatric and psychological consultation.

A pastoral counseling center in Lafayette, Indiana, for example, is composed of four minister-counselors and is served by a panel of consultants including a psychiatrist, a marriage counselor, a psychiatric social worker, a school counselor, an attorney, and a physician. The center functions two evenings a week (7 to 10 P.M.) and one afternoon (1 to 4 P.M.). Recently during an 11-month period the center counseled 52 persons with the following problems: depression (three), marital difficulties (26), religious problems (six), sexual problems (eight), family problems (six), others (three). About 311 hours of counseling were given to the 52 individuals of diverse religious affiliations. Individuals who presented problems with which the pastoral counselor was unable to deal were referred to other appropriate specialists.

Private Practice

The term *private practice* refers, of course, to counselors whose work is not supported by an institution. These counselors are unsalaried and depend on client fees to support their business.

While the exact number of educational and vocational counselors in full-time private practice is unknown, it is believed to be very small—possibly no more than 500 nationwide. The field of psychology is thought to contribute fewer than 5 percent of its graduates to full-time private practice. However, many are engaged in part-time private practice while in the employment of universities, the community, and government agencies. Often counselors involved in full-time or part-time private practice actually provide consulting services rather than the treatment of individuals.

Counselors in private practice engage in diagnostic, evaluating, counseling, consulting, and research activities. They may devote more time to one activity than another, depending on their preparation and interests. Referrals of clients come from schools, physicians, employers, attorneys, social agency personnel, and other private practitioners.

Most counselors in private practice are found in large cities or university towns. The length of their working day varies, but many counselors maintain early morning and evening hours in order to serve clients who cannot come during the regular office hours. Counselors in private practice must work out procedures for accepting cases and spend time getting to know the community in which they practice. The unpredictable work schedules and incomes, as well as the professional isolation from other counselors, demand that counselors who engage in private practice possess considerable emotional maturity and strength.

The American Personnel and Guidance Association has established the American Board on Counseling Services to combat quackery and fraud among those who offer counseling services to the public. Unsavory as the thought may be, it is true that there are a number of "counselors," untrained and unscrupulous, who "counsel" people for a fee. The Board's directory notes that some individuals employed in private practice have offered counseling by mail, "blind" analysis based on tests alone, "memory" courses designed to improve or ensure personal adjustment or vocational success, and a host of other unethical practices.

The American Board on Counseling Services evaluates the policies and practices of individuals and agencies and determines whether they are qualified to meet the Board's standards. Individuals and agencies which meet the standards are listed in the *Directory of Approved Counseling Agencies,* a biennial publication. Counseling services evaluated include (1) counseling for educational progress, (2) counseling for occupations and careers, and (3) counseling for other personal concerns that do not require prolonged or intensive psychotherapy. Approved agencies or individuals receive a certificate with the expiration date of the Board's approval. Currently, the Board is being reorganized into the Association of Counseling and Human Development Services, which will provide leadership to a broader range of counseling services in non-school settings.

In addition to endorsement by professional organizations, many states require professional certification or licensing which includes educational and experience requirements.

Summary

Admittedly, the foregoing description has been very brief. Persons interested in counseling in the diverse settings presented above are urged to seek additional information from the sources cited. As emphasized at the outset of this handbook, no particular profession can exclusively claim the domain of extending help to others; nor can a particular professional group serve all who need assistance. Individuals will continue to seek assistance and advice from any and all sources available when they are troubled. Undoubtedly, innumerable informal sources of help have been overlooked in this presentation; however, it has been our intention to present information concerning the best-known sources of "professional help."

COUNSELING: STATUS AND PROSPECT

CHAPTER 6

The purpose of this final chapter is to present a general overview of the status of counseling occupations. In addition, alternative routes for entry into counseling occupations are presented, as well as some concluding remarks.

Current Status of Counseling Occupations

Examination of Chapters 3, 4, and 5 reveals that today most counselors are employed in educational and other public institutions. But whether the employing institution performs a purely educational or social service function, it has certain expectations for its staff members which are related to its goals. Helping professionals in these settings are employed to contribute to the accomplishment of the institution's goals or mission. For this reason the employment setting inevitably determines, to a large extent, many of the specific tasks performed in the counselor's day-to-day work.

Expectations related to the employment setting place certain demands and constraints on the counselor's behaviors and functions. For example, the fact that many students expect to enter college following graduation from high school requires that the school counselor devote his time to assisting a student in choosing a college and gaining admission to it. Student admission to college is one of the highest priorities of the high school. Thus the counselor may spend most of his time in college counseling even if he might prefer to spend it in personal-social counseling. In short, every setting and the clientele it serves have priorities related to their goals.

In general, the counselor must share and attempt to meet institutional and client priorities. While it is true that priorities may be somewhat flexible, the counselor usually cannot survive in the setting if his personal activity preference is totally divergent from that of the employing institution or his clientele. It must also be kept in mind that public institutions are supported by public funds allocated to accomplish or to serve specific goals. Counselors in public settings are increasingly being held accountable for carrying out the public mandate for the institution's goals.

Autonomy of the individual practitioner is thought by many to be the hallmark of a professional occupation. The true professional's exercise of his autonomy rests with the individual. He does not seek and does not remain in a setting in which he is powerless to alter practices inimical to his professional and personal beliefs. When settings demand unprofessional behavior—required either by shortcomings of the setting, demands of the clientele, or his own inability to make proper use of his training—and when such conditions appear unalterable, the true professional moves on to a situation where such conditions do not exist.

Most preparation programs try to convey to the student an idea of the expectations held by the setting in which he will be employed. These expectations are communicated either directly through instruction or indirectly through the general content and experiences in the program. In short, most training programs view themselves as preparing individuals for fairly specific kinds of employment settings, such as schools, rehabilitation work, etc. Despite this training focus, sufficient common elements exist in the specific training, content, and job demands to enable the counselor to move from one setting to another. For example, he may shift from employment service counseling or school counseling to rehabilitation counseling. Added to this is the fact that personnel shortages have existed in most settings, which in turn have created job opportunities and have contributed to the counselor's mobility.

An examination of the counselor's work in the specific settings described in the three preceding chapters leads to the conclusion that counselors in all settings engage in many of the same activities. Emphasis on specific activities can vary from setting to setting, but certain basic functions appear to be present to a degree in all places of employment. Counselors perform functions that require preparation and skill in interviewing, appraisal of individuals, and counseling. In addition they engage in placement, supervision, and consulting. It must be kept in mind that the type of client with whom these functions are performed will vary from setting to setting, and the degree of emphasis on one activity rather than another will differ among counselors depending on their strengths, interests, and preparation. However, it is rare to find a counselor in any setting who is able to confine his work to a single function. Some counselors would much prefer to restrict their work to counseling, but in most settings the activities required of the counselor are interrelated and basic for accomplishing the goals of the setting.

Current employment qualifications of counseling practitioners require at least a bachelor's degree, and in most settings a master's or doctoral degree is mandatory. Some technical and paraprofessional positions exist which require less education than the bachelor's degree. (This was discussed more fully in Chapter 2 and will be treated later in this chapter in relation to alternate patterns of career entry and development.)

Despite the fact that the past 15 years have been marked by rapid growth in the number, kind, and quality of counseling personnel, major problems have arisen in the field. Many institutions and agencies indicate a need for still more counselors. Most counselors decry the fact that they carry caseloads so heavy that they cannot respond adequately to their clients. The chief factor perpetuating such conditions lies in the shortage of funds. Many institutions and agencies have stretched their resources as far as possible. Simultaneously, they know that they will continue to face an increasing number of individuals demanding service. Funding sources as they currently exist have little in the way of financial reserves left, despite a recognized need for the expansion of services. Whether the solution of this problem lies in the discovery of new financial resources or the realignment of priorities within the institutions is a difficult question.

Accountability, or the requirement to justify expenditures with recognizable results, has become a watchword and an obligation among professionals, especially in publicly funded settings. Most individuals in the helping professions emphasize that the kinds of services provided and the kinds of outcomes sought by counselors are extremely difficult to identify and justify. The product of their work is humanistic, abstract, and highly difficult to quantify, much less "account for." Nevertheless, new counselors in the field should be aware of this situation, and experienced counselors may no longer assume that their services will be automatically funded without some concrete demonstration of their worth.

Alternative Career Patterns and Opportunities

For the young person in search of a professional occupation, counseling has many attractions. It offers opportunities for interesting and highly responsible work, for indeed it is a people-centered profession. Professional counseling work, however, can be entered only after five or six years of college preparation during which time the prospective counselor is urged to secure a broad general undergraduate education followed by specialized graduate education (one or two years) in the helping professions. This basic preparation has long been considered the minimal requirement for entry and advancement as a counseling professional.

Traditionally, the typical career pattern of persons who enter counseling is as diagrammed below.

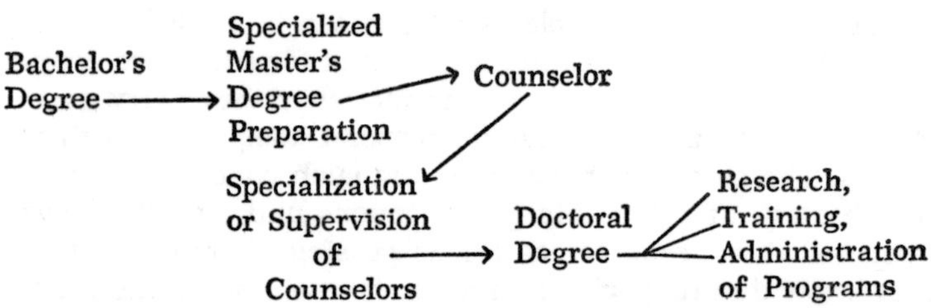

This diagram indicates that one enters the counseling field after extensive training, and that after gaining experience some counselors become supervisors of others or specialists in a particular area of counseling. But it should not be inferred that all counselors obtain advanced graduate education or the doctoral degree. Many if not most counselors, after entering the field and gaining extensive experience, have little interest in obtaining an additional advanced degree or engaging in other activities such as supervision, training, consultation, research, or administration.

Today, attention is focusing on new ways of entering counseling occupations without graduate education or even a college education. Earlier we suggested (in Chapter 2) that paraprofessionals, sometimes referred to as subprofessionals, counselor-aides, support personnel, or technicians, are finding many employment opportunities in some counseling settings.

At least three reasons can be identified for the increasing reliance on paraprofessionals and technicians in counseling. First, there is little hope that the critical shortages of highly trained professionals will be overcome. Second, there is a growing realization that the important ingredients in the helping relationship—sensitivity, empathy, warmth, and respect for others—are human qualities which are widely distributed among the population. Moreover, it is also known that these characteristics are not confined solely to professionals and that they need not be and perhaps cannot be "taught." In short, there is much that people who are not labeled "professionals" can do to help others. Third, other related fields already have set examples in their hiring practices from which much could be learned. For example, it has been recognized for years that ward attendants, despite limited training, are often very influential individuals in the lives of hospitalized mental patients. For these and other reasons, paraprofessionals have begun to be introduced and used in school counseling, employment service counseling, rehabilitation counseling, and many other settings.

The increasing employment of paraprofessionals has led many to envision a future career ladder for counseling personnel vastly different from the traditional pattern. A model for such a career ladder is presented in Table 1, on page 148.

A few observations can be drawn from the career ladder model for counseling occupations presented in Table 1:

1. There is a place in counseling for individuals who want to help others and who have people helping skills but who, for one reason or another, are unable to secure the graduate preparation necessary to become a credentialed professional.

2. It is possible to develop systems for rewarding people for their direct service to individuals as well as for the degrees

Table 1. ***Projected Career Development Ladder for Counseling Occupations***

Level of Employment	Usual Training Required	Typical Responsibilities
Managerial-Professional (Title varies: determined by major function and/or responsibilities)	Doctoral degree plus extensive experience.	Educational, research, consulting, and counseling activities, e.g. education of professional counselors, research director, consultant to agencies for program evaluation and interpretations, agency director, private practice.
Experienced Professional (Title varies: determined by major function and/or responsibilities)	Master's degree plus additional education and/or experience.	All activities cited for professional level plus specialized responsibilities; e.g., supervision and on-the-job training of entry-level counselors and other staff, liaison with other agencies, research responsibility, serving as intra-agency source of referral for "difficult" cases, administrative responsibilities extending upwards to chief administrator in smaller agencies.
Entry-level Professional (Counselor)	Usually, master's degree plus direct or related experience.	Activities involving professional skills and judgment; e.g., counseling, test interpretation, referral, consultation with other professionals, professional evaluations, supervision of technicians and paraprofessionals. Collating and analysis of data, etc.
Technician	Some post-secondary education, plus extensive on-the-job training.	Activities involving some skill and judgment, e.g., group test administration; routine follow-up of clients, maintaining records and information sources, compiling data, outreach activities with clients and employers, collection of initial information from clients and referral sources, etc.
Paraprofessional (Counselor-aide)	Little or no formal post-secondary school education. Mostly on-the-job training.	Usually routine assignments; e.g. test-scoring, clerical activities, record-keeping, data-coding, administrative record maintenance, etc.

they earn and the papers they publish. That is, entering counseling either as a paraprofessional or a professional is not a dead-end job with no opportunity for career advancement and personal development. Individuals who function well in their positions have opportunities for vertical and lateral mobility. As represented in the table, support personnel can become technicians or professionals with the necessary training and experience. It is also true, however, that in most instances vertical career shifts cannot exceed certain levels without specialized preparation.

3. Both the kind and amount of responsibility increase as training and experience are gained.

4. Direct client contact is most extensive at the professional levels of employment (middle employment level), while the extremes tend to have either very restricted client contact or contact that is of a specialized and limited nature. For example, at the paraprofessional and technician levels, direct contact with clients is usually limited to data collection, preparing information about clients, and, in some instances, making information available to clients. However, since jobs at this level are relatively new, additional experience with these personnel may lead to a reassessment of the tasks performed by paraprofessionals and technicians. At the upper levels of employment, administrative and research responsibilities often preclude extensive direct contact with clients except in instances where the job itself involves extending a highly specialized kind of skilled treatment, such as psychotherapy.

5. As indicated in Table 1, it is difficult to specify exact titles for upper-level professionals. For this reason, general titles, such as "experienced professional" and "managerial professional," are used at the upper levels. Titles frequently reflect the functions performed or the responsibilities assigned within a setting. For example, titles at the highest level may include "director of research," "professor," "consultant," "staff psychologist," "director of service," and the like.

6. At the professional level of employment, individuals often are assigned a large amount of responsibility based

solely on their past experience within the setting. While additional training before assuming such responsibility is highly desirable, some counselors and their employers prefer informal, on-the-job training rather than extensive full-time graduate study. Shortages of personnel, particularly at the upper levels, have been a very powerful force in sustaining advancement based on experience alone.

The paraprofessional-technical levels of employment are relatively new to the field. Consequently, their role and function is still evolving. While some guidelines for their employment have been established by professional organizations such as the American Personnel and Guidance Association, there is still a great need for clarification and definition of these positions. All too often, current discussion has revolved around determining what the paraprofessional ought *not* to do. Much of this discussion has originated because of the need of some professionals to defend territorial rights. Constructive refocusing of the discussion should include determination of efficient utilization of both the professional and the paraprofessional within a particular setting as he works with a given clientele.

Opportunities to enter and advance in counseling occupations in the alternative ways mentioned here currently exist to some degree within the general field. In many settings, however, there are few alternatives except entry at the professional level. In other settings, great variability is present; for example, the state of Florida has recently passed legislation which permits the employment of occupational information technicians in school settings. In many private and public settings adherence to professional standards are not strictly observed. For example, some positions with prescribed prerequisite training are filled by individuals who have little if any preparation. Needless to say, this is not a desirable situation, and it raises serious questions about the quality of the setting, the individuals who fill such positions, and the services provided.

Concluding Statement

Much has been written about existing conditions of society that would appear to support the increasing need for persons in the helping professions. Among the social ills cited are loneliness, alienation, interpersonal and intergroup friction, polarization, unhealthy social, economic, and moral changes. These characteristics are viewed by many as contributing to mounting personal stress and difficulty experienced by the individual. Counseling or some other form of highly personalized assistance is often viewed as counteractive to the negative forces in society. It would be presumptuous to imply that the helping professions are the most appropriate counteracting force available. Many of the forces at work in society which create problems for individuals cannot be altered or indeed even modified by counselors. For this reason, persons who enter counseling occupations commit themselves to helping an individual to use his own strength to contend with the forces and situations that impinge on him.

The helping professional can be viewed as one who serves as the facilitator of change, which permits another person to improve his human condition. If the counselor's purpose lies in acting as such an agent, then the quality of his help depends on the kind of person he is, the extent and quality of his knowledge and training, and the degree to which he is able to implement practices consistent with professional and ethical standards.

Given the responsibility assumed by persons who choose systematically to "meddle" in the lives of others, the professional has a great obligation to carry out his efforts at the highest level of endeavor. Competence, caring, and respect for others in large measure are required of him. The counselor who seeks and accepts this responsibility will find much that challenges and rewards him.

INDEX

A K 71